The African Roots of JAZZ

by
Fredrick Kaufman
&
John P. Guckin

2 – 7" – 33 1/3 RPM records included in hard cover edition.
Records also available separately from the publisher. (see page 147.)

Alfred Publishing Co., Inc.

Library of Congress Cataloging in Publication Data

Kaufman, Fredrick
The African roots of jazz.

1. Music–Africa–History and criticism. 2. Jazz music–History
and criticism. 3. Afro-American music–History and criticism.
I. Guckin, John P., joint author. II. Title.

ML3760.K3   780'.96   78-8470
ISBN 0-88284-065-7

I dedicate this book to the
memory of my good friend and
co-author, John P. Guckin, whose
premature death has left us all
with a void that is difficult to fill.

F. K.

CONTENTS

INTRODUCTION

JAZZ – THE ONLY INTERNATIONALLY RECOGNIZED INDIGENOUS AMERICAN ART FORM

A full appreciation of jazz is only possible if one is familiar with the land, people, cultures, and music of West Africa. Seeds were carried to the "new world" through the black slave trade. Later, these seeds were to germinate and mature into a new hybrid art form which has affected the musical taste of our entire planet.

The African Roots of Jazz is the result of over seven years of research carried out in the United States and eleven countries of West Africa. Initial interest in the project was stimulated during a seminar on the history of jazz, which the Authors team-taught during the summer of 1970 at the University of Wisconsin. In the course of this seminar it was realized that there was a dearth of definitive materials on traditional African music and its relationship to jazz. Despite the availability of several books on the history of jazz, little specific field research on the African origins of jazz had been carried out. Since no previous author had simultaneously utilized contemporary technology in his field research, nor had any author devoted himself exclusively to this type of study, we felt the irresistible need to undertake this exciting but arduous venture ourselves. On the basis of our previous experience in Africa and a study of the existing literature, we concentrated our field research in a selected geographical area of West Africa.

The experiences which followed exceeded our wildest expectations—academically, intellectually, and emotionally. The tranquility of African villagers bathing in a quiet rain forest stream, the alarming shrill of a mother's "death wail" for her baby, the regal splendor of an African King's court, the almost hysterical exuberance of a joyously colorful "Yam Festival," the fascinating spectacle of a violent and terrifying secret juju ceremonial rite for Legba (Devil God of Fire), all helped us to develop an awareness of and a feeling for the significance of music in African cultures.

Throughout this book, references are made to pertinent prints, recordings, and music notations, illustrating to the layman as well as the professional musician, the relationship of traditional African music to jazz.

Since conceptual knowledge and a personal feeling for the importance of music in Africa is essential, the first four chapters primarily deal with the transplantation of these musical elements to the new world, and in particular, to the New Orleans area. Chapter V deals exclusively with the African musical elements that have had a direct influence in the development of jazz.

The first six chapters of this book establish the strong roots of African cultures in jazz. It then became important for us to consider the impact of the Afro-American culture upon jazz and its effects on America. Therefore, our book concludes with Jazz—U.S.A.

In the June 1973 edition of the "Unesco Courier," the African scholar Akim Euba, Director of the Music and Research Center of the Nigerian Broadcasting Co., published an article entitled, "The Dichotomy of African Music." Professor Euba makes a plea for books to be written on traditional African music, recordings of their sounds, photographing of their instruments, and the music and dance to be taped and analyzed before they all fade into obscurity.

It is our conviction that *The African Roots of Jazz* contributes to the accomplishment of this request and caters to the interest of jazz lovers, and the needs of serious students of jazz and black studies.

This project has been supported and encouraged by:

James E. Cheek, President of Howard University

Music Department of the University of Pennsylvania

A. W. VanderMeer, Dean, College of Education, Pennsylvania State University

History Department of the University of Wisconsin—Superior

College of Arts and Science of SUNY—Geneseo

Roy Wilkins, Executive Director, NAACP

Aelian Fernando, Executive Secretary, USEFCY

Mark Primus, African-American Historical Society, San Francisco.

To our friends on three continents and the assistance of the governments of Benin, Ghana, Israel, Togo and Nigeria, without whose help this book would never have been written, we would like to express our gratitude. Particular thanks are due to Professor John Swackhammer and Dr. Olly Wilson of the University of California—Berkeley. Both read all the chapters in manuscript form and gave us much excellent advice, most of which we have followed.

We wish to express our appreciation to Alice Guckin for many of the fine photographs seen in this book and Florence Kaufman for her proofreading and literary assistance. Finally, my thanks go to Dr. Sandy Feldstein and the staff at Alfred Publishing Company, for their encouragement, enthusiasm and painstaking care in the production of this edition.

Fredrick Kaufman
and
John P. Guckin

About the Authors

John Patrick Guckin (B.S., B.S., M.ED., PhD.) is a true internationalist. He has been a Ford Fellow in International Development, a Fulbright Scholar in Ceylon and a missionary in Nigeria. He has recently returned from Africa where he was a UNESCO expert in Educational Technology. After living in West and Equatorial Africa for four years, he was adopted by the people of the village of Maku, and a traditional chieftaincy was conferred upon him under the title of "the Omela Oha of Maku."

Dr. Guckin was a faculty member at the Pennsylvania State University and is currently on the faculty of the University of Wisconsin, where he is an Associate Professor of Education.

Dr. Guckin has produced and directed films and video tapes for VISTA and UNESCO and has published numerous articles in the field of education and educational technology.

Fredrick Kaufman (B.M., B.M., M.M.) is a recognized composer, conductor, music educator and jazz historian in the United States and abroad. His compositions have been performed by orchestras such as the Pittsburgh Symphony (William Steinberg conducting). Israel Philharmonic (Zubin

Mehta), St. Paul Chamber Orchestra (Leopold Sipe conducting); at international festivals such as the Darmstadt Festival of New Music and numerous college and university concerts and forums throughout the world. He is a former National Teaching Fellow, recipient of the Darius Milhaud Award in Composition and a Special Projects Award from the California Arts Council for his work in Afro-American music. Professor Kaufman has travelled and studied extensively in West Africa. In addition to writing books, teaching, composing and conducting, he is very much in demand as a guest lecturer at colleges across the United States.

Before coming to Eastern Montana College where he is currently chairman of the music department, he was on the faculty of the University of California-Extension Division (Berkeley), taught at the Rubin Academy of Music and the Hebrew University in Jerusalem, Israel and the University of Wisconsin—Superior. Professor Kaufman's jazz background goes back to the 1950s when he played trumpet with the Sauter-Finnegan Orchestra, Les and Larry Elgart, Sammy Most, Sam Donahue and studied with such jazz giants as John Lewis and John LaPorta at the Manhattan School of Music. His music can be heard on the jazz Blue Note label of United Artists.

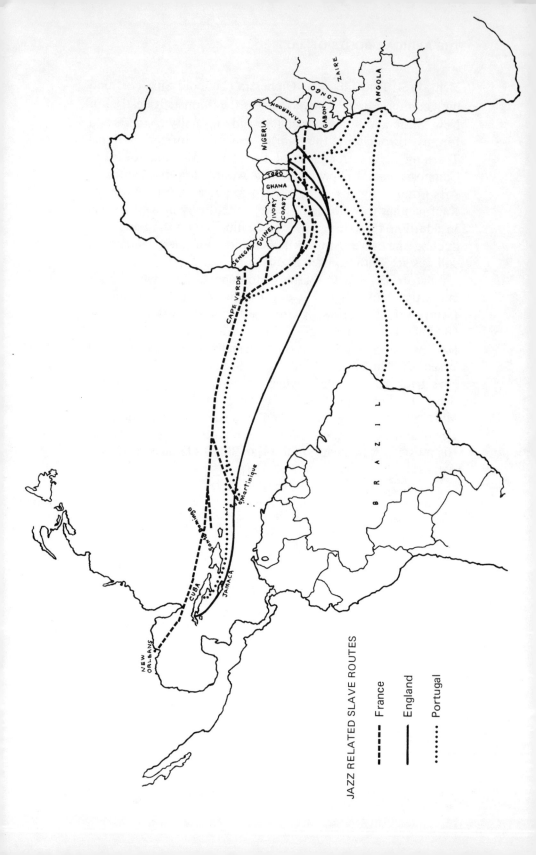

JAZZ RELATED SLAVE ROUTES

France ‑ ‑ ‑ ‑

England ———

Portugal ·······

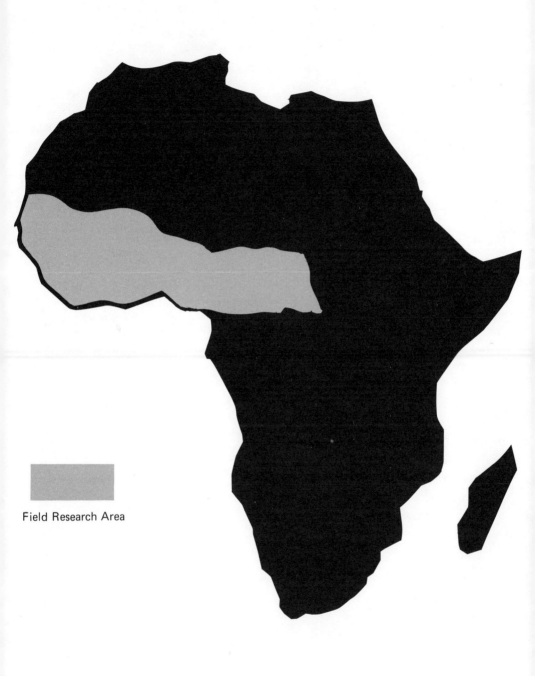

Field Research Area

1

THE
BEGINNINGS

The black races have not contributed positively to
any civilization.

Arnold Toynbee, Historian

The above misconception is due to a gross ignorance of
the grandeur and complexities of African cultures. In order
to understand and appreciate the intricacies of the heritage
of the black American and jazz, a direct intimate association
with traditional Africa is essential.

For hundreds of years music has been and continues to
be, a dominant influence upon the African. Consequently,
it is not surprising that black slaves arriving from Africa and
the West Indies into the New Orleans area carried their

musical heritage with them. The development of jazz is a direct outcome of this transplantation.

The first recorded instance of slave hunting by raiding European pirates in Africa was in the year 1442, when 12 slaves were captured and brought to Lisbon by the Portuguese. The African infidel was also considered fair game for the noble Christian knights of Europe who looked upon their venture as a crusade in the name of God. The sanctioned holy atrocity perpetrated upon the black man had begun. The unconscious philosophical hypocrisy of these predatory forays is sadly a matter of proud record:

> Then might you see mothers forsaking their children and husbands their wives, each striving to escape as best he could. Some drowned themselves in the water, others thought to escape by hiding under their huts; others stowed their children among the sea weed, where our men found them afterwards, hoping they would thus escape notice . . . And at last our Lord God, who giveth a reward for every good deed, willed that for the toil they had undergone in His service they should that day obtain victory over their enemies, as well as a guerdon and a payment for all their labour and expenses; for they took captive of those Moors, what with men, women and children, 165, besides those that perished and were killed . . .
>
> Thus did Europe first bring the "glad tidings" to the African.[1]

Strange as it now seems, slavery was practiced by Africans even before the intrusion of the Europeans. However, the attitude toward a slave was quite different. To the European, a slave was inert property, who had no human status or legal rights and was merely considered a talking implement to be exploited. It was not even considered a crime for an owner to kill his slave.

In Africa, while the slave's legal position was not much better, his treatment by his African master was. He was regarded as a member of the family. He had some rights and it was doubtful that he ever would be sold. If he displayed military or managerial ability, he could rise to a prominent position in the household. Some slaves even became generals or senior administrators.

Who were the slaves?

They were people born into slavery, enslaved as a penalty for a crime, a compensation for a family dispute, or retribution for a defaulted debt. Some were kidnapped, some were given by subject people as tribute to powerful rulers, but by far the greatest proportion were captives taken in wars.[2]

An example of kidnapping as a traditional form of justice can be found in Arachuku, Nigeria. Accused criminals were forced by the village chief and juju (witch) doctor to enter a tunnel called the "long juju," a lurking bastion of retribution to evil-doers. When viewing the long juju today, one cannot help conjuring up images of the intrigues and agonies of the events associated with it. As the mortified victim faced this black hollow abyss which was to determine his destiny, his fear was intensified by the stark reality of the fate of many of his brothers before him. Alone, he entered the tunnel to be enveloped by this empty enigma. If he returned, he was innocent. If guilty, it was announced to the villagers by the appearance of blood in a spring which flowed from the tunnel. Alas, many were called and most were chosen. Inside the tunnel lurked a hidden band of men who chained the hapless victim, slit the throat of a goat or sheep and released its blood into the spring. The preconvicted bewildered human being was then dragged through a secret exit to join others of his lot in a waiting canoe. They were then transported down the winding Cross River through the dense moss laden mangrove swamps and delivered to a slave ship in the lagoon.

The early impact of slavery in Africa and Europe was small. Initially, it was fashionable to have a black slave as a personal servant. As the demand for such human luxuries was limited, the first slaves were only a small part of the ship's cargo.

The economic basis of the slave trade began with the Spanish colonization of the West Indies. In 1510, royal orders were issued for 50 slaves to be sent from Spain to the island of Hispaniola (Haiti and the Dominican Republic) in the Caribbean. The first direct delivery from Africa to the West

3

Indies took place in 1518. Slavery rapidly became a major economic enterprise.[3]

In the 16th century, the number of slaves imported to the Americas was 274,000, rising to 1,341,000 in the 17th century.[4] The 18th century saw a further expansion in the demand for slaves through the agrarian development in America. By 1750, there were 70,000 slaves being imported annually, a figure which increased significantly by the end of the century.[5] From 1451 to 1870 a shocking grand total of almost 10 million human beings arrived in the New World in bondage.[6]

More significantly, for this study of the development of jazz, was the influx of slaves into the New Orleans area between the mid-18th and 19th centuries. At the time of the Louisiana Purchase in 1803, the population of New Orleans was approximately 10,000, half of whom were black. The ethnic impact of this influence is even more apparent when it is realized that in a period of just two years (1775-76), 3,500 slaves arrived in New Orleans.

To appreciate the composition of the slave population of New Orleans, one must consider that this area was alternately ruled over by the French and Spanish for the first 85 years of its existence. Their supply of slaves came from marshalling centers in their Caribbean colonies or directly from Africa, and were predominantly composed of Nigerian and Dahomian (Benin) tribal groups.[7]

G. W. Cable who lived in the New Orleans area during the pre and post Civil War era, identified 18 different tribal groups in a vividly enthusiastic description of the local slave population in an article written for Century Magazine.

> See them . . . tall, well-knit Senegalese from Cape Verde, black as ebony, with intelligent, kindly eyes and long, straight, shapely noses; Mandingoes, from the Gambia River, lighter of color, of cruder form, and a cunning that shows in the countenance, whose enslavement seems specially a shame, their nation the 'merchants of Africa,' dwelling in towns, industrious, thrifty, skilled in commerce and husbandry, and

expert in the working of metals, even to silver and gold; and Foulahs, playfully miscalled 'Poulards,'—fat chickens—of goodly stature, and with a perceptible rosy tint in the cheeks; and Sosos, famous warriors, dexterous with the African targe [light shield] ; and in contrast to these, with small ears, thick eyebrows, bright eyes, flat, upturned noses, shining skin, wide mouths and white teeth, the Negroes of Guinea, true and unmixed, from the Gold Coast, the Slave Coast, and the Cape of Palms—not from the Grain Coast, the English had that trade. See them come! Popoes, Cotocolies, Fidas, Socoes, Agwas, short, copper-colored Mines—what havoc the slavers did make—and from interior Africa others equally proud and warlike: fierce Nagoes and Fonds; tawny Awassas; Iboes, so light colored that one could not tell them from mulattoes but for their national tattooing; and the half-civilized and quick-witted but ferocious Arada, the original Voodoo [juju] worshipper. And how many more! For here come, also, men and women from the great Congo coast—Angola, Malimbe, Ambrice, etc. . . the most numerous sort of negro in the colonies, the Congoes and Franc-Congoes, and though serpent worshippers, yet the gentlest and kindliest natures that came from Africa.[8]

Most of these tribes came from what is known today as Dahomey (Benin), Togo, Nigeria and Ghana. Since it is estimated that over 50% of the slaves who were shipped to the Caribbean and New Orleans were extracted from this region (see map),[9] we utilized Cable's essay as an important resource in our selection of the field research area for our expedition in West Africa.

Testimony to the days of slavery can still be seen in Ghana's great stone forts such as Christiansborg, Anomabu, Dixcove, Cape Coast, Elmina, etc. (see plates 1-4 and map). These old monolithic European slave fortresses can be observed as far north as Guri Island where an impregnable castle commands the entrance to Dakar, Senegal.

Underneath these castles, ancient black cannons still dominate the surrounding area (plate 5). Slaves from various tribal groups were stored in dark, dehumanizing, musty, bat-infested, subterranean dungeons (plates 6, 7). From these

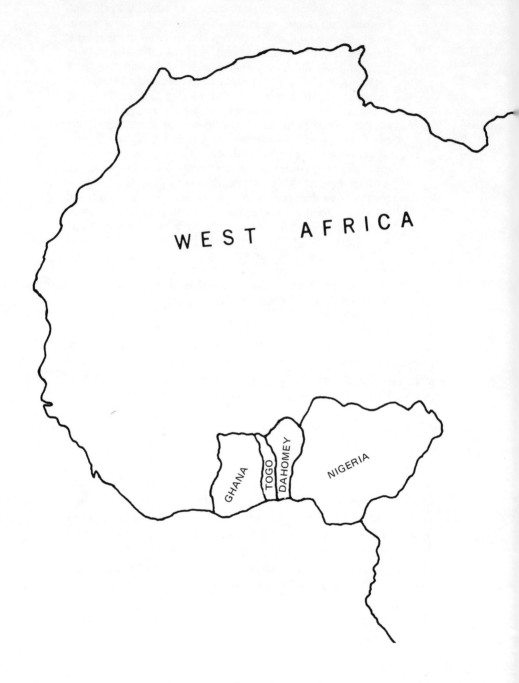

WEST AFRICA

GHANA
TOGO
DAHOMEY
NIGERIA

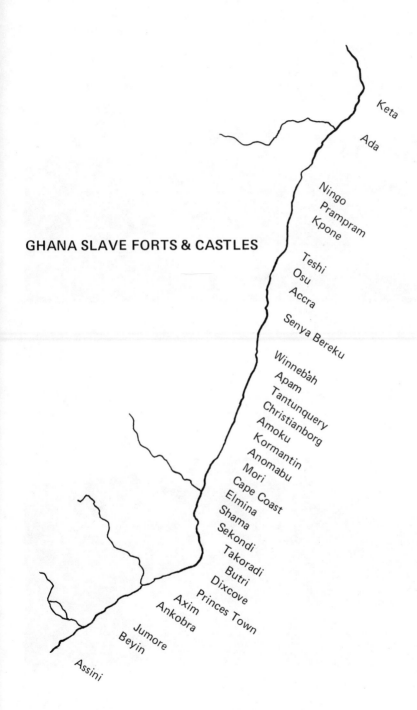

GHANA SLAVE FORTS & CASTLES

Keta

Ada

Ningo
Prampram
Kpone

Teshi
Osu
Accra

Senya Bereku

Winnebah
Apam
Tantunquery
Christianborg
Amoku
Kormantin
Anomabu
Mori
Cape Coast
Elmina
Shama
Sekondi
Takoradi
Butri
Dixcove
Princes Town
Axim
Ankobra
Jumore
Beyin

Assini

Plate 1. *Slave forts and castles*

Plate 2. *Slave forts and castles*

Plate 3. *Slave forts and castles*

Plate 4. *Slave forts and castles* 9

Plate 5. *Cannon*

Plate 6. *Dungeon doors*

Plate 7. *Dungeon*

Plate 8. *Corridor between dungeons*

11

dungeons they were led through dripping, slime-covered tunnels, chained and loaded into long boats for transport to awaiting slave ships and their "middle passage" to the Americas (plate 8). The ocean journey from Africa to the slave marshalling centers in the Caribbean is commonly referred to by historians as the "middle passage."

It was under this circumstance that the initial blending of various African cultures began. Torn from the security of their sacred extended family, denied the support of their tribe, the advice of their fathers and the love of mother, spouse and children, the newly captured slave was forced to seek comfort in relationships with his brothers in bondage. (The West African extended family is a marital structure in which the primary relationship and obligations of the husband are to his parents and family. Also, he has firm commitments to the family of his wife. The wife's primary loyalties are to her family. However, there are numerous variations of the extended systems in different African ethnic groups.) They turned to their music as a common mode of expression and communication. Their mutual plight enabled them to transcend ancient inter-tribal hatreds and competitions. Through the introduction of their music to each other, began the religious, linguistic and philosophic amalgamation, which later was to take root in the new world as a unifying entity.

When visiting Elmina Castle, we were struck by the spacious, comfortable living quarters of the Europeans in sharp contrast to the murky dungeons of the slaves below. The female slaves' quarters were conveniently located directly beneath that of their white master. His religious chapel was on the floor above him. Over the doorway of his house of worship we read the following inscription, "Make ye first a house for the Lord." Ironically, in spite of the plush quarters of the factors (European administrators of the fort), their lives in the forts and castles was so degenerating that their average life expectancy was not more than six months once they reached these outposts of hell. Tropical diseases, alcoholism, debauchery and suicide plucked away many a young life.[10] Neither physical conveniences nor God spared him from his inevitable fate—"the white man's graveyard" (plate 9).

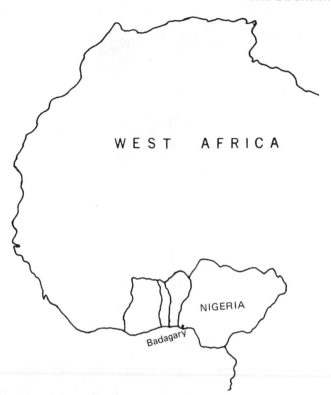

WEST AFRICA

NIGERIA

Badagary

Plate 9. *Quarters of Administration*

13

Plate 10. *Wrist irons*

Plate 11. *Lip clamp and neck irons*

Plate 12. *Monument to Chief Sunru Mobee*

Plate 13. *Metal water trough*

15

Adjacent to these forts massive slave markets developed. Trading also took place in markets assembled along the coast by African Chiefs. We visited one such market in Badagary, a picturesque quiet village on a beautiful lagoon near the south-western border of Nigeria. Here, in the mid-19th century, Chief Sunru Mobee held slaves captive in neck, wrist and leg irons, while they awaited their inevitable sale to the dreaded white slavers (plate 10, 11, 12). In the interim, Chief Mobee used the slaves to work the fields of his sugar plantation. At dawn the blast of a small cannon summoned the slaves from their sleep. They fed from a huge common metal trough and were herded into the fields where they labored under the sweltering tropical sun all day (plate 13). At dusk another cannon blast announced the end of the work day. They were then fed and caged in the slave compound for the night. Those caught eating sugar cane were brutally punished through the horrendous use of the grotesque lip clamp. With the violent eruption and stench of burning flesh, a sharp white-hot metal pin pierced and seated a hole through the clamped lips of the screaming victim. A padlock was then forced through the protruding lips, sealing the mouth and creating a living symbol of the justice awaiting those who disobeyed.

> All slaves when they reached the coast were closely shaved and well annointed with palm oil to give their skins a smooth and glossy appearance, so that it was often no easy matter to tell an old man from a young one. They were then carefully examined by the surgeons, who looked at their teeth, made them jump and thoroughly over-hauled them from head to foot in order to exclude the aged and infirm or any who were diseased, who were invariably rejected, while those who were passed as fit were immediately branded on the right breast with the purchaser's mark to prevent the risk of substitution. In the case of the Royal African Company the letters D. Y. (Duke of York) were used. This was done with a heated silver or iron brand after first annointing the skin with a little oil. When the slaves had all been marked, if no vessel was already waiting, they were confined in the slave rooms of the forts until an opportunity occurred to ship them to their final destination.

The experience of a surgeon on board a slaveship was described in these words:

> "Some wet and blowing weather having occasioned the portholes to be shut and the grating to be covered, fluxes [diarrhea] and fevers among the Negroes resulted. While they were in this situation, my profession requiring it, I frequently went down among them, till at length their apartments became so extremely hot as to be only sufferable for a very short time. But the excessive heat was not the only thing that rendered their situation intolerable. The deck, that is the floor of their rooms, was so covered with the blood and mucus which had preceded from them in consequence of the flux, that it resembled a slaughterhouse. It is not in the power of the human imagination to picture a situation more dreadful and disgusting. Numbers of the slaves had fainted, they were then carried on deck, where several of them died, and the rest were with difficulty restored. It nearly proved fatal to me also."[11]

When the surviving slaves of the "middle passage" finally reached the Caribbean (Haiti, Martinique, Dominican Republic, Cuba, etc.), they were unloaded, "seasoned" (the process of breaking the slave to obey and work for his master), put to work, or stored for transfer to New Orleans. It was during this period that the significant blending of the music of various tribes intensified. The juju (witchcraft) practicing Arada and Yoruba tribes of Dohemy and Nigeria (elaborated on in Chapter IV) dominated this integration and sharply influenced the musical sounds of the Ibos, Senegalese, and Congos.[12] The slaves were either retained in European Caribbean colonies or shipped to New Orleans and South America. Each of these three groups interacted with various types of western music and from a common African base developed their own musical forms—jazz in New Orleans, steel bands in the Caribbean, and the samba in Brazil. In turn, they were later to influence each other. Jazz flirtations with the idiom of Latin-American music which Jelly Roll Morton characterized as the "Spanish tinge" for example,[13] was only the beginning of a courtship with latin music that included

the rhumba and conga in the 20's and 30's (Cab Calloway — *Doin' the Rhumba* and Duke Ellington — *Caravan*) and the samba in the 40's. Immediately after the conclusion of WWII, two distinct styles of Afro-American dance existed in the United States. One was jazz and the other Cuban. The Cuban bands or as they were then called, "Gringo Latino" bands, generally played watered down interpretations of Cuban music and were led by popular musical personalities such as Xavier Cugat and Machito. These bands were primarily made up of imported first class Cuban musicians, many of whom left these orchestras, set up their own bands and concentrated on Spanish-American audiences.

In 1946, the jazz and Cuban sound started to merge, resulting in what was called Afro-Cuban music. Leaders of this music were Stan Kenton and Dizzy Gillespie. One of the first Afro-Cuban jazz works was recorded by the Kenton band in 1947 entitled "Machito," which made full use of the drummers and Cuban rhythms from the Machito band. Kenton was so excited about this sound that he completely reorganized his band, employing musicians such as guitarist Laurindo Almeida, the Brazilian musician who later teamed up with Stan Getz to produce another Latin-American fusion, the Bossa Nova. One of Kenton's best works during this period was his exciting and brilliant arrangement of *The Peanut Vendor*.

In 1947, Dizzy Gillespie, one of the leaders of the bebop movement, excited the music world when he introduced the fantastic Cuban immigrant conga drummer Chano Pazo, to the jazz scene in a New York City town hall concert. That evening is considered by many jazz fans as the beginning of the Afro-Cuban jazz period. Pano mesmerized a captive audience for over 30 minutes as he produced brilliant rhythmic sounds while chanting at the same time in a West African dialect. Pazo, whose grandparents were African,[14] came to Dizzy from the Lucumi religious sect of Cuba, a Neo-yoruban cult whose roots stem from western Nigeria and whose songs can be understood by Yoruba-speaking Africans. As a result of the excitement Pazo generated, the most famous bebop drummers in jazz went overseas to study—Max Roach to Tahiti and Art Blakely to Africa. Mambo bands became the craze of America with "Gahunti"[15] bands filling the dance floors of ballrooms from coast to coast. Blakely went on to become very involved in Afro-American music and became one of the early leaders in this movement. He produced an album called, *Holiday for Skins* in the early 60's, and later on in that decade an excellent and important recording called, *The African Beat*. In *African Beat*, he employed African and American musicians playing music entirely composed by Africans.

These early efforts were the forerunners of an incipient, authentic Afro-American jazz movement, which is currently underway. Until recently, the lack of knowledge and understanding of African music, produced a number of superficial recordings under the guise of Afro-American music. However, since the beginning of this decade, there has been sincere interest on the part of blacks to discover the innumberable vestages of their rich musical heritage. This propensity has inflamed an intense interest in Afro-American music, which we believe could very well become the next dominant musical direction of jazz.

NOTES

1. E. D. Morel, *The Black Man's Burden* (Modern Reader Paperback, New York and London, 1920), pp. 15-16.

2. G. T. Snide and C. Ifeka, *Peoples and Empires of West Africa* (Thomas Nelson and Sons, Ltd., London, 1971), pp. 208-09.

3. Snide and Ifeka, *op. cit.,* p. 210.

4. J. F. Ajayi and M. Crowder, *History of West Africa,* (J. W. Arrowsmith, Ltd., Bristol, 1971), Vol. 1, p. 259.

5. Snide and Ifeka, *op. cit.,* p. 211.

6. Ajayi and Crowder, *loc. cit.*

7. Marshall Stearns, *The Story of Jazz* (Oxford Press, New York, 1962), pp. 38, 40.

8. G. W. Cable, "The Dance in Place Congo," *Century Magazine* (Feb., 1886), p. 522.

9. Philip D. Curtine, *The Atlantic Slave Trade* (The University of Wisconsin—Madison, 1969), pp. 165, 170.

10. Issac S. Ephson, *Ancient Forts and Castles of the Gold Coast* (Ilen Publishing Co., Ltd., Accra, 1970).

11. Ibid., p. 64.

12. Marshall Stearns, *loc. cit.*

13. He used the "Spanish tinge" very effectively in the early stages of jazz with his band the Red Hot Peppers in works like *Jelly Roll Blues.*

14. Marshall Stearns, *op. cit.,* p. 28.

15. The popular mambo bands were made up of 3 to 5 trumpets and a large assortment of rhythm instruments including Conga drums, bongos, timbales, trap drums, vibes, claves, maracas, wood blocks, cow bells, etc., piano and string bass.

Urhobo Sculpture

23

2

THE
ROOTS

West Africa —

Land of:

lateritic [red decayed rock] potholed roads
constant pursuit of insects by red headed lizards
ever present vultures: soaring, walking and waiting
families of wandering pigs, cattle, and goats
scratching chickens everywhere
grasslands
virgin beaches
luxurious futuristic hotels
laterite mud huts with thatched roofs
high rise apartments
open wood and concrete markets
bustling expanding urbanization
open air elementary schools
modern universities
open sewers
willowy coconut palms
lush vegetation of the three storied rain forest
brilliantly colored eight inch millipedes
hanging woody lianas (vines)
mammoth red sun-baked ant hills
mangrove swamps
terrifying darting green mamba (snakes)

and, above all . . . SOUND!

Yes, sound plays a dominant role in the function of all institutions of African societies. Kings are crowned; babies are born; men work; couples marry; victories are won; defeats are accepted; crops are harvested; and people die, all to the accompaniment of the appropriate musical sound.

These musical sounds were frequently not appreciated by early Europeans who colonized Africa. They found the complexities of African music alien, irritating, or boring and often characterized it as noise. One African scholar explains this misunderstanding:

> People unfamiliar with African traditional music, and hearing it out of context, sometimes find it too repetitious. But the more clearly the listener can understand the music's function, the less is likely to be his irritation, until eventually he realizes that repetition is one of the primary aids the music utilizes in order to fulfill its purpose.[1]

To the African, complex musical rhythms are meaningful and expressive. The cross rhythms of various instruments played against each other develops an intense exuberance which is evident in the mutual excitement generated between the musician and the audience.

This total involvement can only be appreciated in light of the knowledge that not only his philosophy of life, but communication itself is influenced by and expressed in terms of the musical elements of tone, pitch, and rhythm found in conversational African languages.

In Yoruba, a folk song must be sung to the tonal inflection of the words. This relationship of words to tone inflection is so important in Yoruba that even the definition of a spoken word is often changed and made meaningless by a slight alteration in the tones. The ● is for a short note, the ▬ is for a long note. Their placement on the 3 line staff represents their approximate pitch.

25

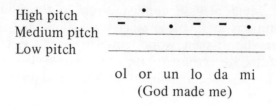

ol or un lo da mi
(God made me)

With the accent on 'da', it changes to:

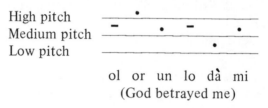

ol or un lo dà mi
(God betrayed me)

Other examples of various meanings of the same Yoruba word are:

jó — dance, burn; jò — leak
kò — hang, learn, not; ko — write, crow, cry;
kó — refuse
wá — search; wà — dig, paddle, exit, come
mí — breathe; mì — shake, swallow

In writing the African language, three alphabet tonal marks must be added. The letter "o" (pronounced "oh") is changed to "aw" spoken as a stacatto note, as in awkward, by writing it "ọ". "´" represents a rising tone and a "`" represents a drop in the tone.

In Ibo the same word can have up to five different meanings. For an example, listen to the word "Akwa" on the first section of the recording (side 1, band 1).

Obviously, pitch and accents are essential to spoken communication in African languages. This finding brought us to an interesting deduction based on the Whorfian Hypothesis which states:

Actually, thinking is most mysterious, and by far the greatest light upon it that we have is shown by the study of language. This study shows that the forms of a person's thoughts are controlled by inexorable laws of pattern of which he is unconscious. These patterns are the unperceived intricate systematizations of his own language— shown readily enough by a candid comparison and contrast with other languages, especially those of a different linguistic family. His thinking itself is in a language in English, in Sanskrit, in Chinese, and every language is a vast pattern-system, different from others, in which are culturally ordained the forms and categories by which the personality not only communicated, but also analyzes nature, notices or neglects types of relationship and phenomena, channels his reasoning, and builds the house of his consciousness.[2]

Very simply, the individual's language structures his understanding of reality. Considering these views of Whorf on language, we developed the following corollary:

Because tone, pitch, and rhythm are essential ingredients to communication in African languages, reality is conceived in musical terms.

Hopefully this corollary will lay to rest the notion that there is an innate genetic musical inclination or aptitude in the black man. We suggest that any musical propensity in the black race is not genetically bound but cultural in nature.
The African "Weltanschauung"[3] is structured by music. Therefore, the dominance of musical art forms in the major events of his life (birth, death, work, happiness, sadness, coronation, execution, etc.), can only be fully appreciated in terms of these aspects of his values and communication systems (plate 14). This system includes instruments as a vehicle of communication.

In consultation with African musicologist Felix C. Mwuba about the use of the nglenge (xylophone) as a communication medium, we learned:

"It is a very important instrument among the Ibo. In addition to its cross rhythm use and as a member of a tradi-

27

Plate 14. *Fishermen chant as they work*

tional orchestra, it also is used to send messages to people in other villages. The musical message is sent at night and travels as far as three or four miles to nearby villages."

We heard specific musical examples associated with this type of communication in the village of Igun, situated in the midst of the beautiful primeval Nigerian rain forest. They were played, sung, and explained to us by members of the Urhobo tribe (record: side 1, band 2).

Songs are composed about everything. In Margaret Green's book on the Ibo of Nigeria, an extreme example is given which demonstrates this point through a story of how justice is meted out in a small village. When a woman is suspected of stealing from another member of the village, all of the village women are called to stand in judgment. They are summoned to the home of the accused by the following song:

> Women who will not come out in this place,
> let millipedes go into her sex organs,
> let earthworms go into her sex organs.

Green goes on to say that this is not a song to be taken lightly, and that its object is to induce the women to turn out en masse.[4]

The following verbatim dialogue between co-author John Guckin and members of the Ibo tribe illustrates the importance of music in ceremonies under the extended family structure.

Jack: Are there any musical ceremonies or festivals associated with birth in your culture?

Mary Mbah: Yes, after the traditional breaking and eating of the kola nuts, the women normally sing and dance. They don't like any man to be nearby because their songs pertaining to birth are very vulgar. They demonstrate (through song and dance) all of the art (love making). They demonstrate the way they behave before the child comes out. If they see the father, they will embarass him.

WEST AFRICA

NIGERIA

• Igun Village

Cyril Eneh: They pour mud, or whatever they can lay their hands on, and pepper him with the tapioca they have made, just to say that he is the scoundrel who did the job.

Mary Mbah: They sing, they dance, they have special songs. If you see them demonstrate, you will be ashamed.

Jack: Ashamed?

Cyril Eneh: Jack, I tell you, you won't believe it. They sing, "Mbia mbia kamma nole, mbia mbia kamma nee te." That is, "Where is the sex act best, it is best in bed."

Mary Mbah: The more they sing, this their song, the more they demonstrate their skills.

Consistent with the importance of music under the African extended family system, sons frequently continue in the profession of their fathers. However, when a talented young boy from a non-musical family wishes to initiate a musical career, his father contacts the master musician who either accepts or rejects the boy as an apprentice. The accepted boy takes daily lessons using the master's instruments and, if successful, eventually purchases his own (plate 15). After many years, if the young musician becomes successful, he repays the master musician for his training with small gifts of money or food from his earnings.[5]

Among the Aka of Ghana, the selection and training of the apprentice drummer is most interesting:

> Because the post of the master drummer of the state was in the past never to be vacated, boys were trained to assume the post in the event of the death of their fathers. Fathers, however, did not always show a willingness to teach their children because they feared that they would be hastening their own departure from this life if they trained people to succeed them. Accordingly, some drummers delayed personal instruction until late in life, or else got some other people to teach their children . . . In the past, however, the training of the state drummer was seriously undertaken. Early in the morning he was taken to the drums and instructed in the art

31

Plate 15. *Musicians and apprentice*

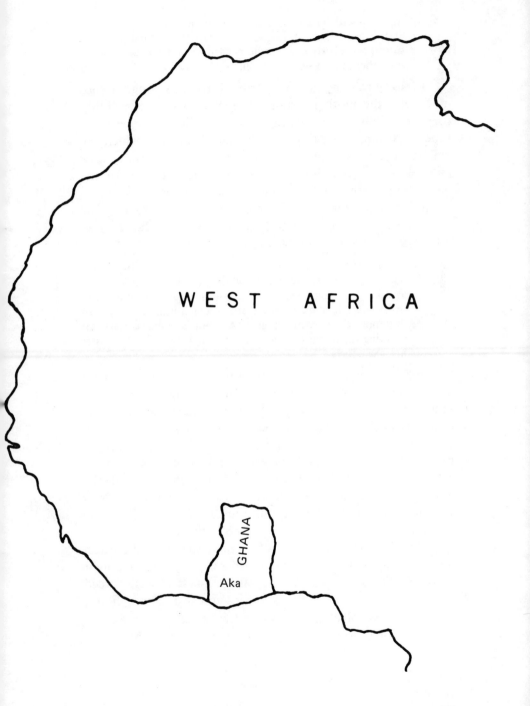

WEST AFRICA

GHANA

Aka

together with other prospective drummers. He was always in attendance when the master drummers played and gradually gained the experience that he needed to step into the shoes of his father in the event of his illness or death.[6]

Types of training vary from tribe to tribe. Among the Ibos of Nigeria the mother assumes a great deal of responsibility for her child's early musical education. She occupies their time by clapping, singing and playing rhythms to which the children dance. Within the Mandingo tribe of Senegal, young men usually train with their fathers, uncles or one of the older men of the tribe. Training goes on for many years, as the musician's profession is both demanding and exacting.[7]

Cudjoe, in his book on the Ewe of Ghana, shows us an interesting and novel approach to education:

> Less talented persons are made to lie on the ground bare backed and face downwards while the master musician sits astride them and beats the rhythms into their body and soul. There is a less drastic method which usually consists of imitating the rhythm orally. A third method consists of allowing the pupils to repeat on his own drum what the master musician plays.[8]

Until recently there was no written notation in Africa and this rote imitation technique of learning was the only mode of instruction available. It seems reasonable to assume that this ability to "play by ear," which undoubtedly contributed to the development of improvisation, was brought by the slaves to the New Orleans area and came to the public's attention in the late 19th and early 20th centuries with the development of jazz. Most of the black musicians in the New Orleans area could not read music until the 1920s. With the enactment of the color code of 1889, the Creoles of color (people whose ancestors were of French, Spanish and African lineage) lost their jobs playing in opera, symphony and light classical orchestras and for the sake of survival were forced to perform with their black cousins uptown. Through this interaction, the black jazz musician learned to read music and was introduced to new European harmonies and instruments.

On the other hand, the Creoles, who until around 1874 had a very respectable role in society and received the benefit of formal musical training, could not improvise at all and had problems adjusting to the black man's music. Alan Lomax, in an interview with Creole musician Paul Dominguez, quotes him as saying:

> See, us Downtown people [Creole], we didn't think so much of this rough Uptown [black] jazz until we couldn't make a living otherwise . . . If I wanted to make a living, I had to jazz it or rag it or any other damn thing . . . [Buddy] Bolden [a trumpet player who, at the turn of the century, was considered by many as the first jazz musician] cause all that. He cause these younger Creoles, men like [Sidney] Bechet [clarinet] and [Freddy] Keppard [trumpet], to have a different style altogether . . . I don't know how they do it. But goddam, they'll do it. *Can't tell you what's on paper, but just play the hell out of it.*[9]

These abilities of the early American black jazz musician are also found in the present day traditional African musician, who must have an exceptionally good ear, an excellent sense of timing, a good memory, and great powers of observation.[10] Consistent with the Creole experience, the present status of the African musician varies sharply from time to time and place to place. Among the Ibo of Nigeria, the instrumental soloists, and especially those who play the oja and ekwe (Chapter VI on Musical Instruments), are well respected and generally well rewarded. Honors accorded to the choral leader among the Ibo is analogous to that of the English minstrel of ancient days.[11] In Ghana, the Ashanti consider the drummer close to God and, therefore, treat him with great reverence, dignity and respect.[12] In Egbaland, Nigeria, and indeed throughout other areas of Africa, we discovered that the livelihood and the status of the traditional musician is generally dependent upon the good-will of the chief or king. He is a member of the court and his services must be readily available for any given occasion.

This has not always been the case. Even though a large number of musicians were supported by the state during and before the days of slavery, many were and still are self-supporting through their music. They roam the countryside (just as today's road bands do in America), and are hired by small tribal groups which cannot afford musicians in residence. However, many wandering musicians now complain bitterly about the lack of financial support for their services.[13] In the past, traditional musicians worked full time at their profession; currently, this is primarily true of only the non-traditional professional high-life (calypso-type pop music) and the rock and hotel society musicians who obtain employment in the larger cities.

Our negotiations for the hiring of musicians was usually long and tedious and we found that it sometimes went on for hours. The musicians we came across had acute business minds. They didn't stop negotiating until they were convinced they had achieved the best financial arrangement possible. Once negotiations were completed and the price paid, the ceremonies began. Each company is a closed economic unit and monies are distributed on an egalitarian basis among its members.

In Igun, Nigeria, the Urhobo Chief treated his musicians with respectable deference in our presence and was very careful to stay out of all musical discussions and financial negotiations that took place. Initially, the master musician never spoke to us directly, and it was necessary to deal through intermediaries in order to reach a mutually acceptable agreement. Usually, our first offer was declined or accepted with some hesitation, and frequently two or three proposals and counter-proposals were passed back and forth between us.

There are several combined factors which affect the prestige of the musician: seniority, instrument played, and various tribal/cultural values. In some tribes, the musician or "griot," as he is called, has a low status but one of great importance. He is allowed to be an eccentric and he takes full advantage of it.

> The gewel (griot) had the right to mock anybody and could use insulting language without any action being taken against them. If a reward for their praises was not forthcoming or considered insufficient, they were liable to switch to outspoken abuse, a consequence of which they were greatly feared and normally amassed considerable wealth. In the past they had a reputation for drunkenness and licentiousness and were long resistant to Islam.[14]

In spite of the African griot's eccentricities, he performed recognized essential functions:

> Griots are by tradition attached to families; they are family jesters and buffoons . . . whose duty is to keep the company amused; they are the family bards, who learn and recite the family and national history . . . they are family magicians (and musicians), who must be present at all ceremonies and whose advice must be taken; they are the first to hold the newborn babe and the last to touch the corpse; they are the actual recipients of most gifts given to their patron; they are the spiritual mentors and guides of the young . . . they console the mourner and comfort the downcast with their merits, triumph and wealth on public occasions; they are lower than the meanest servants and often richer and more powerful than their master. [15]

The griots form a caste within the larger tribal society, are restricted to marriage within their caste, and prohibited from formal participation in any religion. They arouse feelings of both contempt and fear.

Socially recognized groupings of musicians are not only representative of Africa, but appear in many cultures.[16] In Brazil for example, the Afro-Bahian drummers form their own social groups, giving each other special personal names, creating their own musical games and in general are drawn together by the international brotherhood most musicians feel from the magic of their mutual musical creativity.[17] This special feeling is so strong among many of the musicians throughout the world that they have created their own communities and villages, with places such as Greenwich Village in New York City, the West Bank in Paris, Ein Hod in Israel, etc., becoming internationally known as artistic retreats.

37

These elective, segregate characteristics of artists are, of course, also found in Africa. Therefore, the similarities in the status and eccentric life styles of some African and American musicians are not surprising. For example, the beboppers, in the United States, like the griot, were both rebels and held in contempt. They and their followers isolated themselves from the public at large—psychologically, physiologically and socially.

The bebop era started as a black rebellion against "establishment" jazz of the 40s (swing era). The word bebop in itself has a negative connotation. It is derived from the Spanish word "arriba," meaning to "raise up." Originally, the movement was called "rebop," which was later adulterated to bebop.

The beboppers, led by Dizzy Gillespie, Charlie Parker and Thelonious Monk, were rebelling for a number of reasons. They were upset with what had happened to an art form that they as black musicians had given to America. They saw the importance of improvisational solos (the basis of jazz) diminish and take a "back seat" to the big band sound of the swing era. They were angry with the lack of racial sensitivity in requiring them to fight the so-called "yellow-skinned Jap" (World War II).[18] They felt it was a white man's

DIZZY GILLESPIE

picture used by permission of Willard Alexander Management

war and resented the hypocrisy of saving the "free world" in a racially segregated army. They were also angry with the financial and social back seat imposed upon them relative to the white bands, and vented their anger in unusual ways.

As with the griots and other African musicians, who wear brightly colored clothes and ornament their bodies and instruments with jewelry and talismans, the beboppers also had a flare for the unconventional. They wore polka-dotted bow ties with small lightbulbs in the center that would light up at will, pegged pants with double saddle stitching down the sides, pistol shaped rear pockets, berets, etc. Much of their esoteric venacular has become a permanent part of the American-English vocabulary (example in Chapter 8).

Like his African counterpart, the bebopper demonstrated extreme behavioral patterns. Frequently, he would turn his back on the audience and ridicule them through a combination of his music and movements. Therefore, it was not surprising that society reacted by rejecting the bebopper's eccentric ways of life and his music.

Bored with the standard blues pattern, the beboppers enriched chords with extensive use of 9ths, 11ths, 13ths and polychords. In addition to picking up the tempo in most tunes, they made great use of 16th notes and triplets in their solos. The jazz repertoire also underwent a radical change, as many bebop artists improvised new tunes on the chords of existing melodies. Alto saxophonist Charlie Parker, for example, revised "How High the Moon," which he renamed "Orinthology."

While sometimes rejected in their respected cultures, no one can doubt the importance of the musician to society. He performs essential functions. Could there be a wedding without "Here Comes the Bride," a military funeral without "Taps," or an inauguration without "Hail to the Chief"? Similarly, music is essential to African social, economic and political life. In Abeokuta, Nigeria we were to witness and record a regal king's court and chief's council, which typified the emphasis of music in important African affairs.

NOTES

1. Akin Euba, "The Dichotomy of African Music," *Courier Magazine* (UNESCO, Paris, June 1973), p. 26.

2. Benjamin Lee Whorf, *Language, Thought, and Reality* (Cambridge, Mass., Massachusetts Institute of Technology, 1964), p. 252.

3. "Weltanschauung" is a German philosophical term which connotes an individual's view of the world and his environment.

4. Margaret M. Green, *Ibo Village Affairs* (Sedgwich and Jackson, London), pp. 199-206.

5. S. D. Cudjoe, "The Technique of Ewe Drumming and the Social Importance of Music in Africa," *Phylon #16* (Atlanta U. Press, 1953), pp. 280-91.

6. J. H. Kwakena Nketia, "The Role of the Drummer in Akan Society," *African Music* (1954), pp. 39-40.

7. Iolia Nikiprowetzky, *Les Griots du Senegal et Leurs Instruments,* Paris: Radiodiffussion Outre-Mer Ocora.

8. Cudjoe, *op. cit.,* p. 284.

9. Alan Lomax, *Mister Jelly Roll* (Duell, Sloan and Pierce, New York, 1950), pp. 15-16.

10. Cudjoe, *op. cit.,* p. 284.

11. G. T. Basden, *Among the Ibo of Nigeria* (J. B. Lippineatt, Philadelphia, 1921), p. 190.

12. R. S Rattray, *Ashanti* (Clarendon Press, 1923). We made the same observations at the Keemasi Art Festival in Ghana.

13. S. F. Nadel, *The Black Byzantinium* (Oxford University, London, 1942), pp. 301-02.

14. David P. Gamble, "The Wolof of Senegambia," *Western Africa,* Part XIV (London, 1957), p. 45.

15. Geoffrey Forer, *African Dances* (Faber & Faber, London, 1935), pp. 55-56.

16. Alan Merriam, *Anthropology of Music* (Northwestern University Press, Evanston, 1954), p. 142.

17. Melville J. H. Herskovits, "Afro Brazillian Cult Life," *Musical Quarterly, #30,* 1944, 1479-92.

18. Marshall Stearns, *The Story of Jazz* (Oxford Press, New York, 1962), p. 221.

Plate 16. *His Royal Highness — Oba Lipede I*

3

EGBALAND

During the August dry season, our search for sound brought us to Abeokuta, Nigeria, where we experienced an exciting series of events that provided us with a personal opportunity to examine the significance and institutionalization of music in the African society.

We had discovered that the best way to be introduced to the African societal structure and its relationship to music was through social interpersonal relationships. We made this type of acquaintance with an African gentleman at the Abeokuta Sports Club, a vestige of British imperialism which has become Africanized. We explained our project to him and communicated our desire to record traditional African music. Imagine our absolute amazement when he picked up the telephone, dialed "1," and was suddenly in conversation with the Alake (King) of the Egba people. The king graciously extended an invitation for us to visit him at his quarters that very day. We were then advised as to the proper royal protocol and required dress. Our fantasies became a reality as we set out on a totally new adventure to the palace of His Royal Highness—Oba Lipede 1, Alake of the city of Abeokuta and ruler of Egbaland (plate 16).

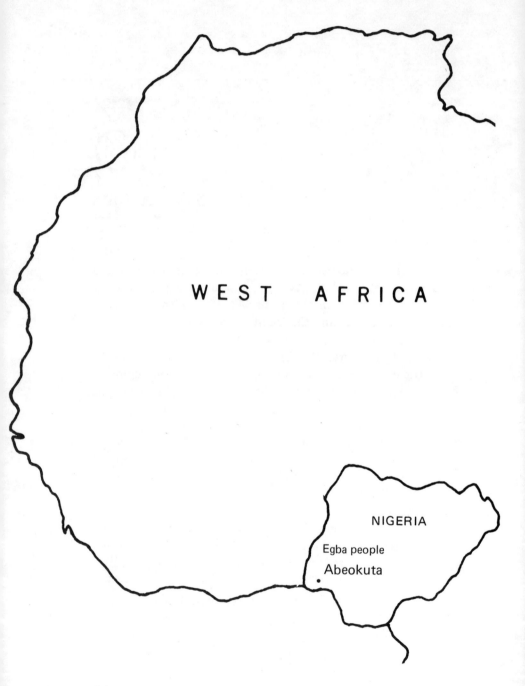

WEST AFRICA

NIGERIA

Egba people

Abeokuta

Winding, narrow streets leading to the road of the palace were naked of trees, crowded with honking taxis and trucks that forced their way through the congested traffic, and perferated with the stench of garbage and dung from open sewers. As we stopped for lunch and gorged ourselves on egusi soup and pounded yam, our senses became immediately alerted to the alien sounds of haggling women in a market place reminiscent of the casbah of Istanbul, the shuck of Jerusalem, and the pushcart-lined streets of New York City's lower east side. Egusi soup and pounded yam, incidently, are considered an African delicacy. Custom requires that the pounded yam be rolled into balls with a millipede-like movement of the fingers against the palm of the right hand (the use of the left hand is considered vulgar). The ball is then dipped into the thick egusi soup, a combination of palm oil, hot chili peppers, a spinach-like egusi vegetable, all prepared on a meat stock of African rabbit (the giant West African cane *rat.*)

On the palace grounds we drove through a beautiful grove of spreading mango trees and were impressed with the apparent ease felt by the local citizens comfortably strolling about. Africans with whom we spoke took great pride in their King and the democratic procedures used to enthrone or, if need be, dethrone him.

We entered the arched portals of the palace walls, and were met by the protocol officer who ushered us into a long, ornately decorated, heavily furnished receiving hall. The palace itself was a large yellow rectangular shaped compound in the 19th century colonial Afro-Anglo style. It housed the royal court, quarters for the Alake's personal wind band, office space and the official residence of the king.

The furniture within the receiving hall was a mixture of two eras, with contemporary chairs and couches scattered among traditionally hand-carved and brightly painted wooden "chief's stools." Two objects dominated this dark green room: a life size portrait of the Alake in traditional dress and a huge pendulum wallclock from the Black Forest of Germany. Pictures of the 1972 coronation of the Alake adorned the walls. A stuffed crocodile lurked menacingly in the corner, and numerous hand carved wooden figures stood in somber silence. We were formally seated in this impressive chamber and anxiously waited to be summoned.

Eventually, we were admitted into the reception room, a long brightly colored hall, covered with Persian rugs and lined with comfortable couches, plush pillows, and totally dominated by the Alake, seated on an elevated throne. We bowed and were most graciously received by His Royal Highness. For the next two and a half hours we discussed everything from our project to women's liberation, Pan-Africanism, art, our individual families and, of course, the Egba culture.

In our conversations, we found the Alake to be a remarkable man. He was completely uninhibited in expressing his opinions, and fully conscious of his authority and its relationship to responsibility.

On the subject of Pan-Africanism he howled, said it was as probable as the United States of Europe and went on to explain that because of the vastness of Africa and the differences between the multitude of ethnic groups, "it would indeed be most difficult."

He was obviously very politically astute, not only locally but internationally. With great pride he discussed both his visit with the Pope and the education of his children at American and Russian universities. His view of women's liberation is typical of the African. In essence . . . THERE'S NO SUCH THING! Appropriately enough, at that moment his wife entered the room and approached to within several yards of his throne. Then, in the accepted manner, she knelt and approached his throne on her knees and elbows. Face down, she spoke to him, then, crawling backwards, departed.

The Alake expressed interest in our project and invited us to attend the royal court of chiefs which fortunately was

Plate 17. *Statue of musician with gan-gan*   47

meeting the next day. This is where, under the Alake's guidance, legal disputes are resolved and policies are established for all of Egbaland.

Throughout our journey, we had been searching for, and eagerly awaiting an opportunity to hear the famous African talking drum, the "gan-gan" (in Ghana called the "danno" or hourglass drum). We were delighted to hear that on the next day His Royal Highness, while seated in his second floor throne room, would learn of each chief's arrival via the sounds produced on these instruments in the court-yard (plate 17).

Early the next day we set up our equipment in a corner of the courtyard and awaited the arrival of the chiefs. The musicians, consisting of five instrumentalists, each with his own gan-gan, were already in attendance. In a shaded area, which served as a waiting place for the chiefs, we observed many highly decorative, historically significant, hand carved statues (plate 18).

Suddenly, there was a surge of activity throughout the courtyard as frenzied drumming began, joyously announcing the arrival of the first chief. Each successive entrance was greeted and announced in the same joyous fashion. A con-versation then ensued between the chief (verbal) and the master musician on his gan-gan. This conversation was often extensive and always ended on an exuberant note (record: side 2, band 1.)

The musicians set a unison rhythmic pattern as the master drummer played cross rhythms to them. Even though the cross rhythms appeared at specific moments relative to the basic pattern, they were completely improvisatory (record: side 2, band 2). We were thrilled to witness this preserved zygote of jazz. The chiefs demonstrated their satisfaction and pleasure with the musicians by placing a coin on the forehead of the master musician.

Following a period of silence, we were startled by the blaring sounds of a huge herald trumpet that overwhelmed the undulating drums (plate 19). The Alake had appeared (plate 20). A throng surged forward and genuflected at his feet.

Plate 18. *Abeokuta palace art*

Plate 19. *Herald trumpet announces Alakes arrival*   49

Plate 20. *Alake enters*

Plate 21. *Inner courtyard*

His Royal Highness, who was dressed in a brilliant white and gold robe and wore a large bejeweled ermine crown on his head, led the procession to the royal court with great pomp and circumstance. He was shaded from the sun by a giant green and white umbrella, the colors of Nigeria. The entire entourage followed in his footsteps to the jubilant accompaniment of the musicians (plate 20, 21). The proceedings over which he officiated lasted for more than three hours and were characterized by both seriousness and levity. When the affairs of state were completed, he dismissed the chiefs and quickly retired to his chambers. Had something happened to the traditional musicians of the royal court, it is doubtful that any of the above proceedings could have taken place.

To our pleasant surprise we were then invited to a private concert given in our honor by the personal wind band of the Alake. Seated in a British style gazebo in the midst of brilliant yellow iris, pendulant bouganvillea and shaded by fan palms, the musicians played a rousing version of "Grandfather's Clock" and "I'm Forever Blowing Bubbles." Co-author Fredrick Kaufman "sat in" (on trumpet) in their finale of an obscure British march. The sounds they produced were reminiscent of the raw quality of the earliest funeral brass band musicians. It is interesting to note that immediately after the American Civil War, wind instruments were discarded by the military bands and became available to the black man for the first time. The director of the Alake's Royal Wind Band told us that they had received their wind instruments in the same manner from the British bands when they departed after Nigeria's independence. With no formal instruction in these exotic instruments, they both experimented and developed their own techniques, styles and sounds (record: side 2, band 3). Compare the music of the Royal Wind Band with that of Bunk Johnson's Brass Band (New Orleans) playing *Didn't He Ramble* (Folkways Record No. FJ2803) and the similarities become obvious (record: side 2, band 4).

Fred Ramsey, in his book *Jazzmen*, refers to the word 'loud,' frequently used to describe the trumpet sound of New Orleans' first known jazz musician, Buddy Boldens, as really meaning: a quality of hoarseness, being unharmonious, and a new approach to playing.

> Buddy was louder than Louis Armstrong with the microphone turned on.[1]

We were astonished to discover the same characteristic brass sounds in Africa. Ethnomusicologically speaking, our experiences at the Alake's palace had to be one of the most exciting of our careers. The phenomenal improvisational drumming of the master musician on his gan-gan, the musical conversation between the drummers and the chiefs, the honor of a private concert of the Royal Wind Band, all whetted our appetite to further explore the relationship of music to other areas of African life.

The next morning we departed for Sagpata, Dahomey— our exploration of witchcraft was about to begin.

NOTES

1. Marshall Stearns, *The Story of Jazz* (Oxford Press, New York, 1962), p. 70.

Plate 18. *Abeokuta Palace Art*

4
WITCHCRAFT

Isn't it ironic, yet fascinating, that the first recognized sounds of jazz evolved from the secret supernatural cults of West Africa?

"Are you leaving, Paschal?"

"Yes sir," he said factually.

"Isn't it early?"

"I must return to Emekuku well before dark."

"Why?"

"We are hiding in our homes by night. A girl was chased by head-hunters yesterday."

"Why are the head-hunters out?"

"Before he died, a juju doctor of another village said that his soul would not rest until the head of a man and woman were sacrificed to him. His people have paid the head-hunters." Paschal left.

Two days later a Nigerian newspaper reported the discovery of the headless bodies of a man and woman. This is not a totally uncommon occurrence in West Africa. In every city, village, or mud hut, whether among the Ibo, or Yoruba of Dahomey and Nigeria, or in the Ga, Ewe and Ashanti areas of Ghana and Togo, the name of a juju god or cult is always heard. In Abeokuta, Nigeria, for example, sits the famous monolithic land mark Olumo Rock (plate 22). This hugh rock with its foreboding crevices and dark caves became a shrine after the Yoruba-Dahomey wars of the 19th century.

The Dahomian wars had raged for hundreds of years. Their empire was surrounded by the Ashanti, Egba, Benin, Ayo and Ewe. As an inland domain she waged constant defensive wars to protect herself from invasion and conquest. To defend herself she also engaged in aggressive wars in order to secure more defendable positions.

In 1727 Agadja, a Dahomian leader, organized an elite army of "Amazon" virgin warriors. For over 100 years this army was maintained, finally falling to French cannons in the early part of the 19th century. As a counter defensive measure to Dahomian invasions, the Egba people sought the protection of juju when under seige.[1]

With the city of Abeokuta under attack, an Egba witch-doctor was called upon to cast a spell on Oluma Rock, evoking the help of the spirit from within. Under this juju spell, enemies who pursued the Egba people into their sacred sanctuary fell under the curse which would cause their skin to ooze blood and pus.

As the Dahomian army charged, the Egba fled to the rock to protect themselves from the impending onslaught (plate 23). Realizing that there was a curse on the rock the entire Dahomian army turned and fled. Even today, many Africans of other tribal groups refuse to venture up into the rock for fear of their lives.

Under and in the rock are three chambers. One is used to store drums (gan-gan) and the other two are for prayer (plate 24). At specific times during the year sacrifices are made to their gods, as they continue to pray for protection. Dried brown blood stains give mute testimony to the sacrifice of goats and black cows which are offered to the spirit on various occasions. Originally, small children were captured

Plate 22. *Olumo Rock*

Plate 23. *Olumo Rock crevice*

Plate 24. *Steps to instrument room*

and sacrificed. This practice has been abandoned with the substitution of sacrificial roosters. Incidentally, it is believed that these rites originally functioned to extend the life of the Alake. The rooster is also used in voodoo (juju related) ceremonies in the Caribbean.

Some form of religion has probably always existed in the cultures of Africa. In every culture man has endeavored to explain the unknown, control the unpredictable forces which affect his life, and provide for immortality via religion. When different religious beliefs come into contact with one another, an accommodation and synthesis of each other's value systems take place. For example, the use of the Christian cross and medals to ward off vampires, werewolves, devils, etc., in Eastern Europe and the Caribbean, is similar to the adjustment of Mohammedanism and Christianity to indigenous African religions. An American Baptist missionary in the Central African Republic in 1961, states that he drove out devils which had possessed Africans (exorcism rites). When asked if he really believed in demon possession, he said, "The Bible says, 'Satan and his evil spirits shall prowl about the earth, seeking the ruin of souls.' The witch doctors have satanical powers."

In New Orleans there was a unique religious combination of elements that provided an atmosphere for the development of jazz which did not exist in other areas of the country. The slave of the protestant north found it extremely difficult to identify with the Protestant Church, which attempted to obliterate his African heritage. However, in the South, and particularly in Catholic New Orleans, he found commonalities with elements of his juju religion which enabled him to identify with Catholicism. These included sacred statues (idols), medals (charms), the call and response patterns of the gregorian chants, the similar use of ornamentation, pomp, clerical dress, and regal titles.

Since the African worshipped many gods, he readily identified with the Catholic mystery of the "Holy Trinity" in which there are three persons in one God. He could pray to God the Father (patriarch), God the Son (extended family), God the Holy Ghost (juju). This identification further facilitated the assimilation of Christianity into his religious beliefs.

The African capacity for assimilation and amalgamation of various aspects of Western and indigenous culture, particularly religion, exists to this day.

In a recent research survey on this subject conducted by Dr. John Guckin at the Alvon Ikoku College (Owerri, Nigeria) of teacher trainees of the Christian faith, 76% of the students stated that juju was the strongest power on earth next to God. In West Africa each individual god is worshipped by means of specific instruments and a defined repertoire of songs and dances.[2] Improvisation and satire are two of the essential ingredients of jazz which are frequently found in juju songs.[3] The music, instruments, liturgy, dancing, dress, ritual, methods of calling to worship, types of sacrifice and established sacred days also differ from cult to cult.[4]

Some specific examples of instruments used by the Yoruba for worship of different gods are:

Instrument	God
Bata Drum	Shango[5]
Bull Roarer	Oro[6]
Animal Horns	Ogun[7]

The Poro cults of Liberia exhibit a fascinating use of instruments in juju worship. Their nighttime singing is done to the accompaniment of three to five sweet sounding pottery whistles. These whistles come in sets that are pitched a fourth apart, to the accompaniment of a bass note which is produced by the blowing of a huge antelope horn into a large clay pot. This deep bellowing note is always referred to as the "old woman," or the devil's wife. Instead of the pottery whistle, the flute is sometimes used. The tunes are very short, and are played over and over again.[8]

Another variation of a cult associated instrument was demonstrated at Badagary, Nigeria, the former slave market of Chief Sunru Mobee. The people danced, played, and sang for their needs before an oil-filled carved tree stump into which they pounded a sacred metal prayer rod, the symbol for Ogun, the god of iron and war (plate 25).

Our search for the fierce devil worshipping Arada tribe whose practice of juju strongly influenced the slaves in the Caribbean and subsequently the development of jazz in New Orleans, brought us to Sakpata, Dahomey.[9] Warned of the possibility of legal difficulties and cultural hostilities toward the viewing of secret traditional ceremonies by non-Africans, we inquired discreetly as to the whereabouts of the local master musician and were directed to a nearby hut. It must be remembered that even though juju is the well-known secret practice of many West Africans, the subject is a very delicate one. Public performance before non-believers is frowned upon and great discretion is required when inquiries are being made.

Passing through the archway of his compound, secluded by a rust colored mud wall which was topped with jagged glass, we were suddenly struck by the menacing appearance of a carved crocodile looking down upon us. Inside, a profusion of mysterious surrealistic murals covered the walls of the laterite huts.

These paintings of people and animals were accompanied by inscriptions, and what appeared to be dried streaks of blood. Numerous statues had been placed on pedestals and in the grottos specifically constructed to contain them.

The whereabouts of our musician was unknown, and the situation became further complicated by a proliferation of confusing advice in three languages. With each new advisor, we acquired an additional potential passenger until finally we departed with a search party of eight.

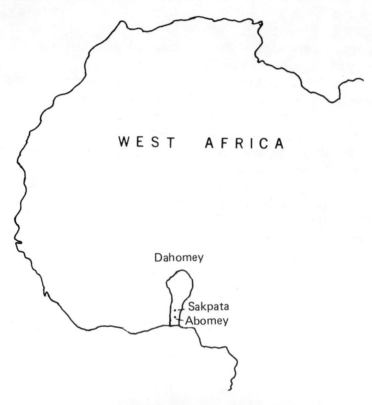

WEST AFRICA

Dahomey

Sakpata
Abomey

Plate 25. *The symbol of Ogun*

On leaving, we walked off in a wrong direction and were suddenly confronted by a crudely constructed shrine of sticks and grass. It housed a two foot statue of a man armed with a huge phallus. He stood before a small platform which contained a shallow depression for sacrifices. We had found Legba, the devil god and the god of fertility (plate 26) worshipped by the Arada and Yoruba tribes. The dominant phallic representation in the idol was obvious. Although we were unable to secure an explanation of the significance of this representation, one might note and speculate the possible relationships between this idol and traditional male dominance and ancestor worship in the African society. It was the Arada and Yoruba tribes, with their gods and music which had a dominant influence on the spread of witchcraft throughout the Caribbean, Brazil, and New Orleans (Cable, cited in Chapter II). In New Orleans the juju of the Arada made major contributions to the development of voodoo secret societies, which eventually were to lead to the establishment of the swinging funeral brass bands. This discovery intensified our excitement, and we returned to the car with great expectations.

Sandwiched between 17 pieces of delicate electronic equipment, our situation began to resemble the congestion of the overcrowded Barnum and Bailey midget car circus act. To compound our difficulties, the farther we proceeded from Abomey the more difficult the roads became. Eventually, we found the musicians in the nearby town of Sakpata. Initially cautious about having their art and culture exploited, the musicians finally agreed to perform when they were convinced of our sincere interest in African traditional music. However, they insisted that protocol and tribal law demanded we first obtain prior permission from King Pomaligni of Abomey before they could proceed. With the equipment set up and protected from dust, rain, sun, and the playful hands of curious children, several intermediaries proceeded four miles to the King's palace where permission was granted. Phase Two in the continuing confrontation with the African bureaucracies (a conglomerate gift of Anglo-Franco coloni-alism) demanded that final approval be given by the mayor, who consented after he was given his usual "dash" (an institutionalized form of bribery which usually takes the form of money or gifts).

Back at the compound, as the musicians dressed them-selves in traditional costumes and performed the purification rites, we stood under the enervating sun, among the sweat-flies of the hot dusty tropics, surrounded by numerous phallic statues of the fertility god, Legba. Darting red-headed lizards, scavenging vultures lurking about, and the rejection of an amorous billy goat by his mate occasionally broke the tension.

After three hours of negotiation, preparation and perspira-tion, the ceremony finally began. The end of the purification rites within the inner compound was announced violently by a fierce and frightening scream made by a demon-like figure who suddenly hurled himself in front of us. Beneath a shroud of shredded white cloth his heavily scarified face twitched spasmodically. His hand clutched a sharpened wooden stake, and his sleek black body, adorned with white spots, underwent a series of menacing wild contortions. He moved erratically in the direction of Legba, and suddenly with a shrill cry threw himself at the foot of the shrine, plunging the stake into the ground (plate 27).

At that moment the musicians appeared in a trance-like state, which seemed to remove them from their physical environment. As they moved into the ceremonial area, they immediately began to play their instruments, most of which were giant gourd maracas and different sized bells of various pitches.

Their widely varied costumes, which included a black stove pipe hat, small brilliantly embellished skull caps, hoop skirts of boldly patterned cloth and cowrie beads, bracelets, labrets (an ornament worn through the lip), earrings, and necklaces, all tended to complement the sounds that were being produced (plate 28).

Plate 26. *Legba*

Plate 27. *Legba worshiper*   65

Plate 28. *Dancers in Sakpata*

The bells, which were attached to the jewelry of the dancers, were activated by the synchronized movements of their bodies which produced a perfect eighth note pattern (♫ ♫) against the occasional improvised cross rhythm of the master musician's gan-gan. The emotionally charged atmosphere created by the total involvement of the musicians in the ceremony became self-generating.

The area was filled with bodies of gyrating dancers, swinging arms and legs of local tribesmen, and the flailing hands of absolutely involved musicians, who were producing a repetitious hypnotic rhythmical pattern that went on for hours. All the above incidents, plus an endless series of piercing screams and shouts were recorded, filmed and video-taped at a moment in time which seemed to have no relation-ship to the present.

Not only does this music have the potential to transcend time, as stated above, but space as well. There is copious documentation of these types of cult ceremonies in the Caribbean (known as voodoo), South America (known as macumba/umbando), and New Orleans (known as vodun). Music, song, and dance are an integral part of all of their sacred supernatural ceremonies.

In Brazil, the macumba Neo-yoruba singing style known as the "candomble," utilizes the African musical ingredients (elaborated on in Chapter V) of the call and response pattern, repetition, polyrhythms, polymeters, falsetto singing and dominance of percussion, and is almost identical to the traditional music of Western Nigeria. Today, the Bahia region of Brazil is a Yoruba religious stronghold. Its capital city, Santiago, has been called the "Rome of the Africans," because Yoruba is spoken at the conversational level in both the cults and Christian churches. Belief in macumba and umbando has become so widespread in Brazil today, that they are practiced in various degrees by black and white Brazilians regardless of their other religious affiliations.

Trinidad is another source of Yoruban secret society cult music, much of which is dedicated to the Yoruban god of thunder, Shango. Originally, drums were used within these ceremonies, however, when they were banned, the Trinidad blacks resorted to using bamboo sticks and tambos. When these also were forbidden, as they were considered to be dangerous potential weapons, the Trinidadians originated the steel band. The only instrument used within these bands (which were to become very popular in the West Indies and the U.S.) are drums of various sizes made from the tops of large steel oil barrels. These are cut to size and heated and hammered into a corrugated instrument capable of producing a wide variety of notes. The yearly festivals in Trinidad have become a great tourist attraction, as large colorful steel bands march through the streets to the sound of the Calypso. Calypso (like jazz) is another example of the result of the West African slave trade. It was to return to Africa and emerge in contemporary African pop music as Hi-life.

In Jamaica, the Obiah cult gets its name from the Ewe word "obia" which means charm. On the exotic isle of Carriacou in the lush Grenadines of the Caribbean, a local dance, strongly Ashanti in origin, also includes words from the Ibo, Mandingo, Arada, and Congo tribes. Another example of the African cultural influence in the Caribbean is a ceremonial healing song entitled "Cariba Dambella Bother Me." Dambella is the name of the Benin snake god.

Haiti has been the site of quite a bit of successful religious amalgamation. Dambella is often depicted as St. Patrick, the saint who allegedly drove the snakes out of Ireland. Ogun, the African juju god of iron and war, is often found on the voodoo altars represented by the warrior Archangel Michael dressed in armor.[13]

Voodoo music in Haiti has the power to possess the dancers through the supernatural use of hypnotic rhythms.[14] In Africa ritual dances have a similar effect on the participants, who either move in a trance-like state or leap violently with wildly rolling eyes.

A similar analogy can be found in some black American church services, where individuals are suddenly saved and "born again." This salvation offers a parallel with the African custom of possession by a god. Christian baptism has its counterpart in the water initiation ceremonies of some African cultures, a factor which aided in converting slaves to the church.[15]

Elements of African religions, music and dance have not been maintained in as pure a form in the United States as in the Caribbean and Brazil. There are several possible reasons for this. In many Latin-American countries the blacks are either a majority or large minority group. Conversely, the U.S. was a "melting pot" of many cultures of which the blacks were only a small part. American blacks lost contact with Africa at an earlier date than did their brethren in Latin America. Finally, nervous slave owners banned the use of drums by their slaves for fear that they would be used to incite slave revolts, which indeed did happen. Without drums, gods could not be summoned.[16] However, the music of cult societies had a definite effect upon the development of jazz in the New Orleans area.

The preservation of these cult ceremonies in the new world assisted displaced slave populations to retain their musical heritage in an alien society. The breakdown of the traditional African extended family established a vacuum in which juju-related secret societies of New Orleans, Haiti, Trinidad, Brazil and Cuba had to assume a greater function in the protection of their members. They provided financial aid and help at times of death, as well as providing entertainment to break the dreary existence of everyday life.

The relationship of the black man's secret society in America to those found in Africa is described by Herskovits in his book, *Dahomey*.

> With elected membership and with ritual secrets in the manner of the American lodges, such groups often have large followings and persist over long periods of time. Their primary purpose is to provide their members with adequate financial assistance so that at the funeral of a member's relative . . . he can make a showing in competitive giving that will bring prestige to himself and to his group. Each member must swear a blood oath on joining, and there are adequate controls over the treasurer. Each society has its banner and indulges in public display of its power and resources in its processions, especially when it goes as a body to the funeral rituals.[17]

None of these funeral ceremonies could have taken place without the prescribed musical rituals.

Since New Orleans secret societies had their origins in Africa, it is not surprising that they provided similar services to their members. Sister Johnson gives a fine example of the importance of these secret societies at funerals in New Orleans in the following statement:

> A woman's got to belong to at least seven secret societies if she 'spects to get buried with any style . . . And the more lodges you belongs to, the more music you gits when you goes

to meet your Maker. I belongs to enough now to have shoes on my feets. I knows right now what I'm gonna have at my wake. I already done checked off chicken salad and coffee.

I'm sure lookin' forward to my wake. They is wakin' me for four nights and I is gonna have the biggest funeral the church ever had. That's why everything I makes goes to the church and them societies.[18]

Sister Johnson's statement obviously reflects a total commitment to life after death and reincarnation, which are indigenous to West African tribal beliefs.

The funeral brass bands were the dominant feature of the New Orleans juju-oriented secret societies and its link to jazz.[19] These bands actually initiated the jazz movement. They were employed by the secret societies at funerals for the sole purpose of adding dignity to the occasion and tribute to the deceased. They marched behind the deceased at a very slow 4/4 tempo, to tunes such as "Come Thee Disconsolate" and "Nearer My God To Thee."

After the burial, a quiet recessional moved from the cemetary, where, at a respectable distance, the band broke into a happy up-tempo tune in 2/4 time, i.e., "The Saints Go Marching In" or "Didn't He Ramble."[20]

It was during these moments that the first acknowledged sounds of jazz improvisation took place. This lively music was designed to raise the spirits of the family and help them overcome their loss. People in the streets generally joined the festivities as they enthusiastically danced, swinging to the brass band's improvised melodies.

These funeral brass bands became so popular in New Orleans that they were hired to play in clubs and brothels for the entertainment of the clientele. Their original instrumentation (trumpet, clarinet, trombone, tuba, banjo and assorted drums) was kept intact. Their repertoire incorporated the blues songs heard throughout the South, the marches they played at funerals and the all important improvisation associated with them. JAZZ HAD BEGUN!

NOTES

1. Karl Polany, *Dahomey and the Slave Trade* (University of Washington Press, Seattle, 1966), pp. 2, 28, 30.

2. M. J. Field, *Religion and Medicine of the Ga People* (Crown Agents, London, 1957), p. 34.

3. M. J. and F. S. Herskovits, "The Outline of Dahomey's Religious Belief's," *American Anthropological Studies* (Banta Publishing Co., Menasha, Wisconsin, 1934).

Also refer to J. H. Kwabena Nketiz, *African Gods and Their Music* (University of Ghana, Accra), pp. 3-8.

4. A. P. Merrian, "Music Bridge to the Supernatural," *Tomorrow's Magazine,* Vol. 5, No. 4, (1957), p. 66

5. I. Laeye, Timi of Ede. "Yoruba Drums," *Odu: Journal of Yoruba & Related Studies,* No. 7 (March 1959).

6. J. Olumide Lucas, *The Religion of the Yorubas* (Lagos CMS Bookshop, 1948), p. 120.

7. E. G. Parridner, *West African Religion* (Epworth Press, London, 1949), p. 81.

8. George Schwabs, "Tribes of the Liberian Hinterland," Peabody Museum Papers, Vol. XXI (Harvard U., 1947).

9. C. W. Cable, "The Dance in Place Congo," *Century Magazine* (Feb., 1886), p. 522, and Herskovits, M. J., *The Myth of the Negro Past,* (Harper and Bros., New York, 1941), p. 246.

11. Macumba and umbando are descendents of good and bad juju of West Africa.

12. Harold Courlander, *Haiti Singing* (Chapel Hill, the University of North Carolina, 1939), p. 5, and Stearns, Marshall, *The Story of Jazz* (Oxford Press, New York, 1962), pp. 24-25, and Boulton, Laura, *Music Hunter* (Doubleday, Garden City, New York, 1969), pp. 445-52, and Roberts, John S., *Black Music of Two Worlds* (Praeger, New York, 1972), pp. 33-35.

13. J. S. Roberts, *Black Music of Two Worlds* (William Morrow & Company, Inc., New York, 1974), pp. 33-39.

14. A. Metrau, *Voodoo in Haiti* (Shocken Books, New York, 1972), p. 189.

15. Roberts, *op. cit.,* p. 166.

16. Ibid., p. 39.

17. M. J. Herskovits, *Dahomey* (J. J. Augustin, New York, 1938), Vol. I, p. 166.

18. *Gumbo Ya Ya,* edited Saxon, Dreyer, and Tallent (Boston: Houghton Mifflin Co., 1945), p. 301.

19. M. S. Stearns, *The Story of Jazz* (Oxford University Press, New York, 1976), p. 58.

20. Ibid., p. 61.

Abeokuta Art

5

MUSIC

In that famous New Orleans vacant lot called "Congo Square," where the Africans danced and sang publicly since the Louisiana Purchase, the music that one heard gradually changed. The repressed blacks were impressed and affected by contact with the melodic music of their rich masters and incorporated it into their playing. The proud and complacent whites on the other hand, disdained the "crude" beauty of the black man's music. The eventual result was an American black art form called jazz.

Unfortunately, little documentation of that crucial 19th century transition period is available. However, the following comments in a letter written in 1880 by musicologist Lafcadio Hearn illustrate the evolutionary process that was taking place during that time:

> I fear I know nothing about Creole music or Creole Negroes. Yes, I have seen them dance, but they danced the Congo and sang a purely African song to the accompaniment of a dry-goods box beaten with sticks and bones and a drum made by stretching a skin over a flour barrel . . . it is precisely similar to what a score of travellers have described. There are no

harmonies—only a furious countertemps [cross rhythms].
As for the dance . . . the women do not take their feet off
the ground, it is lascivious as possible. The men dance very
differently, wildly leaping in the air . . . The creole songs
which I heard sung in the city are Frenchy in construction,
but possess a few African characteristics of method. The
darker the singer, the more marked the oddities of the intonation [the blues pitches, which were so confusing to the white
man].[1]

In contrast to European "art music," both African traditional music and early jazz are an integral part of a complete
societal structure. The word "art" has no counterpart in
African languages. Whenever the word is used it is done so in
the form of some European language. The African musician
deals with dance, music, folklore and costumes as a completely
integrated entity involved in all phases of life including religion,
work, war, birth, death, etc. Similarly, American jazz has
emerged from work songs, field hollers, religious music, folklore and the funeral brass bands of the 19th century black
society.

In "Lippincott's Magazine" of December, 1868, John
Mason Brown traced the following subdivisions among the
music of the southern slaves:

1) Religious songs, e.g., "The Old Ship of Zion," where the
refrain of "Glory, halleloo" in the chorus keeps the congregation well together in the singing and allows time for
the leader to recall the next verse [call and response].

2) River songs, composed of single lines separated by a bar-
barous and unmeaning chorus and sung by the deck hands
and roustabouts mainly for the soul.

3) Plantation songs, accompanying the mowers at harvest, in
which the strong emphasis of rhythm was more important
than the words.

4) Songs of longing, dreamy, sad, and plaintive airs describing
the most sorrowful pictures of slave life, sung at dusk when
returning home from the day's work.

Plate 29. *Juju worship*

Plate 30. *Ceremonial dance*

5) Songs of mirth, whose origin and meaning, in most cases forgotten, were preserved for the jingle, rhyme and tune, and sung with merry laughter and with dancing in the evening by the cabin fireside.

6) Descriptive songs, sung in chanting style, with marked emphasis and the prolongation of the concluding syllable of each line. One of these songs, founded upon the incidents of a famous horse race, became almost an epidemic among the Negroes of the holding States.

In Chapter II we said that the thinking processes of West Africans are in terms of musical sounds. These languages are musical languages and the drum patterns are not just rhythms but talking tunes that tell a story or transmit a message.

Jazz has similar correlative ties between music and language. Because vocal blues existed long before the first Dixieland bands embraced the clubs of Storeyville, it was quite common for most early jazz instrumentalists to imitate a vocal blues line on their instruments. Storeyville has an interesting background. In 1897, New Orleans passed a resolution that established vice segregation resulting in the red light district called Storeyville (named after the resolutions' sponsor Sidney Story). Its famous streets (i.e., Basin Street, immortalized later on in the song Basin Street Blues) boasted of some 200 brothels, nine cabarets, gambling joints, dance halls and honky tonks, and employed over a dozen jazz bands to entertain its customers. One can in all honesty say that jazz grew up in Storeyville. Great jazz musicians, i.e., Jelly Roll Morton, Joseph "King" Oliver, Louis Armstrong, Bunk Johnson, Johnny Noone, Sidney Bechet, Kid Ory, Ma Rainey, the Tuxedo Brass Band, the Olympia Brass Band, and the Original Dixieland Band are just a sampling of the artists who developed their skills in Storeyville between 1910 and 1917 when the Navy Department finally closed it down.

Instrumental *vocalization* was quite important and common within the playing style of early musicians. Trombonist Joe Nanton of the Duke Ellington Band, for example, was literally able to make his instrument talk.

Conversely, the *instrumentalization* of jazz singing has produced a number of outstanding vocalists, including the great blues singer, Billy Holiday, who absorbed the instrumental ideas of Lester Young and others into her singing style; Jack Teagarden whose vocal phrasing was the same as his trombone playing; and of course, the great scat singer, Ella Fitzgerald.

Many historians make the overly simplistic generalization that the rhythms found in jazz stemmed from Africa, and that the harmonies, forms, etc., came from Europe. We found that *every* musical element within early jazz has been influenced by African traditional music.

MELODY

1. Blues

The word "scale" is one of western terminilogy and has absolutely no meaning to the traditional African musician. One of the main objectives of the African composer is the creation of the melody. While definitely concerned with half tones and whole tones (though not in the theoretical sense), he creates his melody with reference to specific focal points. Because most of sub-Saharan Africa has never had its own written musical tradition, we will use staff notation for practical purposes. However, it should be kept in mind that it represents African music and not music based on the absoluteness of the western tempered scale. Due to this musical freedom, he is capable of creating scales of wide variety. This same freedom in which the musician varies his tonal center by placing the stress on moving focal points has been the contributing factor in the production of an abundant variety of melodies.

After 30 years of investigation with more than 100 tribes, South African musicologist Hugh Tracey found that 40% used a five interval scale, 20% a six interval scale and the remaining 40%, a seven interval scale.[3] In the areas of West Africa that were tapped for slavery to New Orleans, 85% of

the musical examples recorded used the five interval pentatonic scale.

The most common five interval scale we found in West
Africa is illustrated below in relation to the European chro-
matic scale. Notes which are to the right of the line are of a
slightly higher pitch.

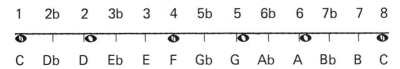

Note that the third or flat third and the seventh or flat
seventh found in western scales are missing. When the slaves
included these pitches in their work songs, they fell midway
between the third and flat third and the seventh and flat
seventh, becoming known as the blues tonalities (or blue
notes). Since the advent of these blues pitches in America
was not originally conceived of instrumentally, but vocally,
jazz pianists often strike both thirds or sevenths together to
gain the blues effect. Randomly choosing the key of C, the
blues scale looks like this: (record: side 2, band 5)

Approximate Blues Pitches

These same blues pitches were used extensively by the slaves
in their songs while working in the cotton, sugar and tobacco
fields of the South. Even though they were forbidden to talk
to each other while working, singing was permitted. This
garbled type of singing, known as "Field Hollers" or "Cries,"[4]
is closely related to African praise songs and "men's songs"
of numerous West African tribes. These sounds became a
means of communication between the slaves in the field and
were a total mystery to their white overseers.

79

One of the outstanding characteristics of the "field cry" is its constant use of the bent tone, either upwards or downwards, or to no tone at all. (Record: side 2, band 6)

Field Cry

Bent notes

This bent note, which has become an integral part of the blues, usually occurred on the third or seventh tone of the scale. This was, of course, the most natural place for the slaves to place it, as these tones did not exist in most African pentatonic scales. It was also quite natural for the African to sing in semi-tones, as musically they were less inhibited than the westerner in these respects.

On occasion we did find the use of the flatted seventh within traditional African music. This might be one of the explanations why the intonation of the blues seventh was slightly lower and more constant than the blues third in very early blues recordings.

The presence of the blues seventh in the South in the 1800s has been substantiated by a musicologist named Thomas Fenner, who prefaced the first edition of his book, *Cabin and Plantation Songs as Sung by the Hampton Students* (1874), the following way:

> Another obstacle to its [the slave music's] rendering [on paper] is the fact that tones are frequently employed which we have no musical characters to represent. Such, for example, is that which I have indicated as nearly as possible by the flat seventh in *Great Camp-Meetin'*, *Hard Trials* and others. These

tones are variable in pitch, ranging through an entire interval on different occasions, according to the inspiration of the singer. They are rarely discordant and often add a charm to the performance. It is of course impossible to explain them in words, and to those who wish to sing them the best advice is that [which is] most useful in learning to pronounce a foreign language: Study all the rules you please, then—go listen to a native.

Jazz musicians were not the only ones to make use of the blues note. In 1923 composer Darius Milhaud wrote a master-piece called *La Creation du Monde.* This work is a fully developed classical-jazz composition that repeatedly uses the blues pitches.

Trombone (Passage in E minor)

Blues note   Blues note

Blues note

2. The Riff

Within the African song a rhythm is established by a group of musicians and is repeated over and over again with the master musician (leader) signaling rhythmic changes and improvising cross rhythms to the repeated pattern. These rhythms may not necessarily correspond to the meter or duration of the song above it, just as the harmony of the jazz riff, a short phrase which is repeated over a changing chord background, doesn't always correspond to the repeated melody.

The riff developed as one of the solutions for playing jazz with big bands. Fletcher Henderson was actually the "witch doctor" who came up with most of the solutions to deal with

10 to 14 musicians playing jazz simultaneously. He harmonized the solo line for full sections (4 saxophones, etc.) while still making use of the African call and response pattern. The phrases which were thrown back and forth between the woodwind and brass sections, became known as the riff. The riff, which characterized the swing era, reached the height of its development with the Bennie Moten (in 1935 taken over by Count Basie) and Benny Goodman bands.

Riff Pattern

The Basie band coined a new phrase called the "head riff." In tunes such as "One O'Clock Jump," the brass and saxophones developed to a fine art the very exciting technique of tossing an improvised unison phrase between sections.

3. The Falsetto Break

The falsetto break, sometimes described as a snap in the vocal chords,[5] and often associated with the Swiss and the American Indian, is also commonly heard in West Africa. While in Noudo Kopo, Togo, in a colorful evening of leaping bodies and intriguing sounds, we heard the falsetto break from a wild figure of a man who leaped into the midst of the dance area with a shocking shriek. His Swiss yodel-like falsetto cry permeated the collage of sounds around him, and was immediately followed by the thunderous answer of the male chorus, evidence that the falsetto break exists in Africa.

The falsetto break, which first appeared in America in work songs, field cries and spirituals, has been maintained both instrumentally and vocally through great performers such as Blind Sonny Terry, Joe Williams with Count Basie, Baby Cox with Duke Ellington, Vera Hall, Tommy Johnson and more recently with Leon Thomas.

Falsetto Break

Blues note   Falsetto break

In our field recordings we noted other African melodic traits which obviously had made the transition into early jazz, namely:

1) The fourth degree of the scale was rarely used.
2) The interval of a fifth was very unusual.
3) The melodic range was never large and rarely exceeded a sixth.
4) The melodic line usually followed a descending pattern.

Close examination of the early recordings of blues singers like Ma Rainy, Bessie Smith, Blind Lemon Jefferson, etc., substantiate the existence of many of these characteristics in jazz. For example, the fourth degree of the scale which is rarely heard in African melodies is also the least used tone of the blues scale. When it is used, it generally functions as an auxilliary tone to help color the third or the fifth.[6]

In all our travels we never heard the interval of a fifth in an African melody. This seems to substantiate Winthrop Sargent's observation that the 6th degree rarely moved to a second in early blues recordings.[7]

The African melodic characteristic of a short range (usually a fourth or fifth) was very common in both the blues and later on in the riff. The English musicologist, Rev. A. M. Jones, who lived in West Africa for an extended period of time, described the African melody the following way:

> Broadly speaking, the outline of an African tune is like a succession of the teeth of a rip-saw; a steep rise (not usually exceeding a fifth) followed by a gently sloping down of the tune; then another rise—then a gentle sloping down, and so on. The tendency is for the tune to start high and gradually to work downward in this saw-like manner.[8]

If we compare Jones' analogy with that of Samuel Charters' findings, the results are astounding. Charters found after analysing the music of 259 blues tunes, that 191 had a similar pattern to that of African melodies. This descending approach, which incidentally is also the African method of singing scales, is not only common to the African melody and the blues, but also the American work song.[9]

Blues

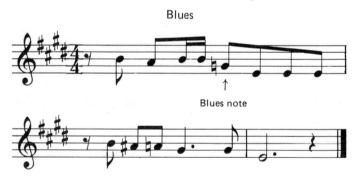

Blues note

HARMONY

Even though it can safely be said that there is no one specific harmony throughout Africa, there are definite patterns to substantiate the findings of similar harmonic interval groupings in different geographical areas.[10] We encountered the use of harmonic intervals on numerous occasions in West Africa.

Examination of the map on page 86, will show that almost all the tribes from Nigeria to Senegal harmonized in thirds or unison. The tribes from Cameroon and parts of Zaire used harmonic intervals of fourths and fifths, most often harmonizing in fourths at the cadential point.

The African's concept of harmony is different than that of the western musician who subordinates harmony to melody. While the African considers the melody of prime importance, the harmonic line is actually an integral part of the melody and therefore he places an equal stress on both notes.

Tribes can be placed into groups on the basis of the specific intervals at which they sing. When a tribal group sang the melody a fourth lower, they never introduced a third. The same was true of groups which harmonized in unison or fifths.

The parallel third groups (it is doubtful that intervals of a third existed in Africa before the arrival of the European) create an interesting harmonic variation to the other interval groups. Because the third groups never use accidentals on the bottom voice, they no longer sing the same melody. Intervals created are sometimes major and at other times minor.

From all appearances, the basic blues chord progression of I-IV-I-V-I, seems to be based totally on European harmonies. However, knowing what we do about the harmonic intervals found in West Africa, and the contention that all the other musical elements of jazz were affected by or derived directly from the African musical heritage, we find it impossible to believe that the early jazz harmonies were in

THE AFRICAN ROOTS OF JAZZ

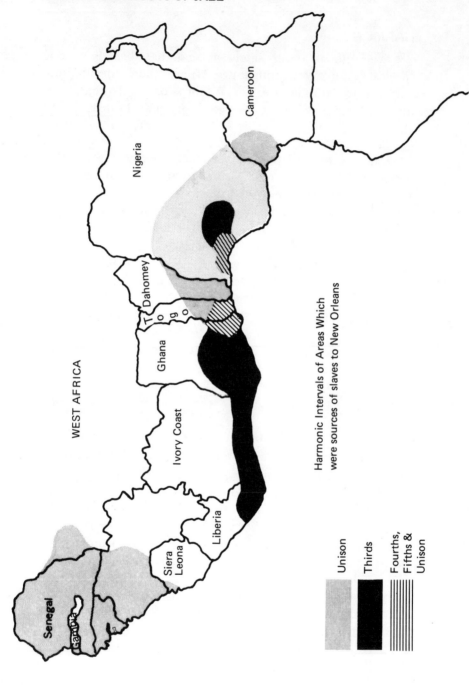

WEST AFRICA

Cameroon

Nigeria

Dahomey

Togo

Ghana

Ivory Coast

Liberia

Siera Leona

Senegal

Gambia

Harmonic Intervals of Areas Which
were sources of slaves to New Orleans

Unison

Thirds

Fourths,
Fifths &
Unison

no way influenced by the African. It is more likely that the early jazz harmonies were a synthesis of two traditions with a dominating European harmony.

Even though both harmonic traditions are based on totally diverse concepts, there are some traditional African musical similarities which can be found in the early blues progression that make the transfer from Africa to the new world almost unchanged. Obviously, the tribes that harmonized in thirds or unison had little difficulty, if any, fitting their melodies to European harmonies. The European tradition of building chords or triads on thirds had been the practice for centuries, and one to which these tribes (which made up the largest grouping of slaves to the New Orleans area) could easily adapt.

Concerning tribes that harmonized with intervals of fourths and fifths, it is quite possible that the blues progression of I-IV-I-V-I is horizontally based on the intervals used by those tribes. In any case, as a result of the previous African use of these intervals, the acceptance of this progression would be a natural transition.

CALL AND RESPONSE

The call and response pattern, which at one time was heard in revival and church meetings throughout the South, can be heard today on radio stations all over the United States. One such meeting has been documented by *Folkways Records* (FJ2801) in their great series on jazz. In this recording we hear Rev. J.M. Gates in an especially inspiring sermon, evoking the call and response pattern as he moves the entire congregation into the valley of Ezekial. These improvised sermons happen in a free manner and develop into a definite form, with the preacher repeating and improvising on his story. While the preacher tells his story, his voice develops a chant-like sound, and the congregation responds to his words in a free flowing antiphony reminiscent of the call and response found in African music.

The call and response pattern can be heard as far back in jazz as the early brass bands of New Orleans and in the recordings of King Oliver and Louis Armstrong (*Mahogany Hall Stomp*—OKEH, 1929) on through Count Basie, Fletcher Henderson, Benny Goodman, and into the 50s with Charlie Parker and Dizzy Gillespie "trading fours." When trading fours, each soloist improvises for 4 measures in constant rotation. Many times the soloist will musically comment on the phrases of his predecessor and sometimes even develop them further.

In Africa there are four types of call and response patterns:

1) exact choir repetition of a soloist's verse,
2) choir repetition of the soloist's refrain,
3) soloist sings the first half and the choir sings the refrain,
4) choir vs. choir.

There are, of course, variations on each of the above patterns.

The vocal technique of the call and response is based on an antiphonal exchange between the soloist and the congregation. Many times the soloist will improvise his part and the chorus will repeat the same phrases, or phrases which are very similar. The scheme of this form is $AA^1 AA^2 AA^3 AA^4$, etc.

We found examples of the call and response in: a darkened Anglican church in Abraka, Nigeria (Uhrobo); a church procession on a road in central Nigeria (Ibo) with over 400 parishioners walking two abreast in multi-colored clothes, led by a reverend and his altar boys, all singing the antiphonal call and response pattern; at a juju cult ceremony in Sakpata, Dahomey (Fon); and literally everywhere we went in West Africa (record: side 3, band 1).

Fanny Kemble's description of a work song in Georgia illustrates the use of the same call and response pattern by slaves in America in 1839.

> My daily voyages up and down the river have introduced me to a great variety of new musical performances of our boatmen, who invariably, when the rowing is not too hard,

moving up or down with the tide, accompany the stroke of their oars with the sound of their voices. I told you formerly that I thought I could trace distinctly some popular national melody with which I was familiar in almost all their songs; but I have been quite at a loss to discover any such foundation for many that I have heard lately, and which have appeared to me extraordinarily wild and unaccountable. The way in which the chorus strikes in with the burden, between each phrase of the melody chanted by a single voice, is very curious and effective, especially with the rhythm of the rowlocks for accompaniment. The high voices all in unison, and the admirable time and true accent with which their responses are made, always make me wish that some great musical composer could hear these semi-savage performances.[11]

RHYTHM

Rhythm is the most acknowledged and certainly one of the most important contributions the African has made to jazz. In order to understand the African rhythmic influences upon jazz, we must know what the indigenous rhythmic music of West Africa sounds and looks like, and what happened to this rhythm by the time the first phrases of jazz came about.

Every facet of the African's music is completely rhythmically contrapuntal and is conceived of in terms of polyrhythmic and polymetric time relationships. The twelve-pulse melodic phrase, which is a very common feature in African music, would probably receive a handclapped accompaniment by the European at the quarter note group:

African Music:

European clapping:

This would almost never occur when an African claps; he would not be interested in clapping such a simple pattern.

The following pattern is one we found within a number of melodies we recorded: (record: side 3, band 2)

Same African music as before

African clapping

The result is a feeling of rhythmic freedom which contrasts with the restrictions imposed on the Westerner to fixed groupings determined by simple rhythmic arrangements. Within contemporary compositions, however, (both in jazz and classical music) this is not necessarily true due to the diversity of approaches.

Africans enjoy creating combinations of different rhythmic patterns. It is not unusual, for example, to hear three (eighth notes) against four with the three dominating: (record: side 3, band 3)

clap

clap

or four against three with the four dominating, according to accent placement.

After close examination of our tapes, certain rhythmic characteristics became apparent. A basic rhythmic pattern was usually set by a majority of the drummers, with the master drummer improvising cross rhythms to these patterns. In some cases the basic pattern was started by one group: (record: side 3, band 4)

and picked up by another group on the 1st, 2nd or 3rd beat of the middle of the first rhythmic phrase (record: side 3, band 5).

The musician thinks and responds to multi-rhythms both horizontally and vertically. To transcribe an African composition with its undulating tension and relaxation points, which are so essential to the dance, it is necessary to understand the multi-dimensional orientation of the music. When we remember that the placement of accents is continuous in both voices, the above example becomes more interesting: (record: side 3, band 6)

The first and second drummers usually continue their rhythmic pattern throughout a composition. Drum ensembles number in size anywhere from two or three to as many as seven or eight. While these patterns continue, the chorus sings a melody with its own rhythmic pattern, and hand-claps an accompaniment to that melody. The master drummer's placement of short accented improvised phrases at other points of stress creates a rhythmically stimulating composition that becomes a total sound experience (record: side 4, band 1).

This custom of clapping to the weak beats of the bar is certainly one which made the transition to jazz. Any jazz musician or fan will tell you that you never clap and snap your fingers on 1 and 3, rather on 2 and 4. Duke Ellington used to do a wonderful routine to his tune, *It Don't Mean A Thing If You Ain't Got That Swing* in which he explained to the audience that one must snap his finger on 2 and 4 in order to be a swinger.

The master musician plays a most significant role in the game of cross rhythms. He is the musician who is constantly improvising. In Abeokuta, Nigeria, we counted 11 varied rhythms as played by the master drummer against his ensemble. It is not only his job to enrich a piece of music with interesting improvised cross rhythms and beautiful themes, but to insert these themes before the dancers show obvious signs of losing their momentum. His rhythms and themes must rejuvenate the dancer at the correct psychological moment. An awareness of the placement of the basic beats in a complex drum ensemble helps the dancer determine which part of his anatomy to move in order to create yet another rhythm pattern.

At the turn of this century, ragtime rhythmic patterns as found in tunes like *The Entertainer* by Scott Joplin still showed a strong resemblance to African cross rhythms.

The Entertainer
Scott Joplin

At the Kumasi Fine Arts Festival in the Ashanti area of Ghana, the Africans' concept of complex rhythms was fully demonstrated to us. The country's finest traditional musicians, dressed in their usual colorful costumes and carrying a spectacular assortment of drums, displayed that unmistakable pride found in Africans. Their performance provided us with one of the most musically satisfying evenings of our entire journey. Unfortunately, it was forbidden to film or record the music and dancers at the ceremony for fear of commercialization or offending the chiefs. However, by this time our eyes and ears were attuned to the culture around us, and we made the following observations of one of the tribal groups:

The Komkomba War Dance

Seated in the center of a large clear area were the following instrumentalists: gan-gan (hour glassed drum), gankogui (bell), atumpan (tenor drum), and a from (bass drum) player. The dancers who lined the back of the enclosed compound were covered with traditional war ceremonial dress. Upon their heads they bore the horns of the roan antelope, held in place by a silver ring laden with cowrie beads. Their bodies were covered with antelope skin and white macramé cord surrounded their waists. Perched on their rumps were the tails of horses, and to complete this picturesque ensemble they carried bows and arrows upon their backs.

The activities were introduced by a constant four-note rhythmic pattern played on the gan-gan. The final note was an undulated upbeat. Pitches on this unique hour glass shaped drum can be varied by increasing the tension of the drum head by squeezing the rawhide cords that surround the instrument and hold the heads in place (see plate 15). This pattern was shortly thereafter followed by another on the gankogui. Led by the plumed gan-gan drummer, the dancers started their procession to the central area. The coordination of the 22 dancers, adorned with cowrie beads on their arms, legs and hips, was superb. One could not hear the sound of a single out-of-place cowrie bead, even for an instant. Within a few moments of the dancers' entrance the musicians had rhythmically mesmerized both themselves and the audience. Their voices were used in unison as a rhythmic instrument at specific moments relevant to the composition and added to the splendor of the moment.

Komkomba War Dance (Ghana)

*Interval of a Perfect 4th.

Even though instrumentalists never ventured far from the basic theme, improvisation occurred sporadically throughout the work (especially on the gan-gan).

Compositions such as this are known to go on for hours, and sometimes even for days. The last sound to be heard as the ensemble ended together was the accented sixteenth note of the chorus—a brilliant end to a most exciting work.

A few days later we heard the same compositions performed by the same musicians. With the exception of the improvised parts, it was almost exactly the same as the previous performance we heard in Kumasi. This should dispel any illusions that traditional African music is not a preconceived work. The Africans' compositions are of a highly creative, relatively free-flowing nature within a firm structure that is still open enough to permit artistic variance.

The following humorous anecdote in Mgbirichi, Nigeria further illustrates the preconceived nature of compositions in Africa. Discovering early in our field trips that the musicians loved listening to themselves perform (as do musicians all over the world), we made it a standard procedure to replay the tapes for them after each performance. The villagers crowded around the speakers after the performance and cheered whenever they heard themselves on the tape. They always knew exactly when they were to enter, and when one of the musicians did not hear his initial entrance, he was aghast. We replayed the tape four times for him and each time he did not hear himself at the exact moment of his entrance; he picked up the speaker and shook it. It took quite a bit of talking to convince him that he was on the tape but that our playback facilities were too small to pick up his delicious deep bass tones.

In the music of Mgbirichi we could feel the Africans' love for cross rhythms and accents. These rhythmic vestiges were preserved in early jazz through syncopation and improvisation. By replacing the polymetric and rhythmic points of stress into the monorhythmic and metric systems, the black man made his adjustment to the white man's music. However, the process was not a quick one. Documentation of the "wild and unaccountable" rhythms found in black American work songs in the 1830s,[12] as well as the difficulties encountered in writing down the rhythms of these songs with normal notation,[13] confirms our beliefs that although acculturation took place, it was a long and difficult process.

Even though polymetric ideas appear in solo jazz choruses throughout the history of jazz, very few compositions have been written in this vein. Stan Kenton experimented slightly along these lines for an unsuccessful period in the 40s in a movement called "progressive" jazz. Most recently jazz trumpet player Don Ellis has been the leader of the important rediscovery of polyrhythm and polymeters. His album *Electric Bath* employs meters ranging from 7 to 13 to 15 and 2 against 3, etc., with extensive use of electronic instruments and free-wheeling jazz choruses that reach a new height in the tune *Turkish Bath*. The 3 + 3 + 2 pattern of other Ellis tunes such as *Pussywiggle Stomp* are "unmistakably African in origin and approach."[14]

Don Ellis

NOTES

1. Robert Goffin *Jazz* (Doubleday, Doran & Co., Garden City, N. Y., 1944), p. 23.

3. Hugh Tracey, "The Development of Music in Africa," *Optima Magazine,* Vol. 14, #1 (March 1964), pp. 48-49.

4. J. W. Work, author of *American Negro Songs* has described the field cry as "a fragmentary bit of yodel, half sung, half yelled." J. W. Work, *American Negro Songs* (N.Y.: Howell, Soskin & Co., 1940), pp. 34-35.

5. H. W. Odun and G. B. Johnson, *Negro Workaday Songs* (Chapel Hill: University of North Carolina Press, 1926), p. 263 ed passim.

6. Winthrop Sargent, *Jazz: Hot and Hybrid* (E. P. Dutton & Co., 1946), p. 166.

7. Ibid., p. 165.

8. A. M. Jones, "African Music in Northern Rhodesia and Some Other Places," the Occasional Papers of Rhodes Livingstone Museum, IV (1949), p. 11.

9. Samuel Charters, *The Bluesman* (Oak Publications, 1967), pp. 18-19.

10. A. M. Jones, *Studies in African Music,* 2 vols., (London: Oxford Univ. Press, 1959), pp. 217-21; also see map on p. 230.

11. Frances A. Kemble, *Journal of a Residence on a Georgian Plantation* (New York: Harper and Bros., 1864), p. 218.

12. Frances A. Kemble, *Journal of a Residence on a Georgian Plantation* (1838-39), (New York: Harper and Bros., 1864) as reprinted by Alfred Knopf, 1961, N.Y., p. 218.

13. W. F. Allen, C. P. Ware, and L. M. Garrison, *Slave Songs of the U.S.* (A. Simpson and Co., 1867, reprinted by Oak Publications, N.Y., 1965).

14. Dr. B. D. Simms and Ernst Borneman "Ragtime, History, and Analysis," *The Record Changer* (October 1945), Vol. 4, no. 8, p. 8.

6

MUSICAL
INSTRUMENTS

The African is extremely versatile in his quest for sounds. His instruments are unique to a specific locale, but many are common throughout West Africa. Frequently, the instruments were adapted, modified, and even renamed.

The following is a cross-section of examples we found throughout West Africa, many of which are the forefathers of contemporary Western musical instruments.

Ababiala

This very popular instrument of West Africa is found in various sizes. It is constructed from the trunk of a coconut palm, is frustrum shaped and is a single-headed instrument. It can most often be heard within the traditional orchestra or as an accompaniment instrument.

This is a single-headed barrel shaped drum with a penetrating sound. It is made from a hollowed-out hardwood tree and is frequently ornamented with various carvings. The desired pitch is achieved by varying the tension on the strings which are attached to pegs. The Ewe version is quite large, supported

by a stand and closely resembles the Conga drum of the Caribbean. It is frequently played by the master drummer who varies the pitch by simultaneously using his hand and a drumstick on the head. It can be heard in the traditional orchestra or in the chants accompanying warrior parties.

Asafo

The atumpan is an extremely important talking drum of Ghana which is found in the Ga-Adangbe, Ewe, Dagomba, Mampursi, Gonja and Wa areas. The drum shell is made from the solid log of the cedar-like tweneboa tree (the Senegalese use the wood of the red kola tree). As it was believed that a powerful spirit lived inside the tweneboa tree, an egg is offered in sacrifice before cutting it down. Even today drummers can be seen pouring a libation on the drum before it is played.

Atumpan

The Danno is a double headed, hour glass shaped talking drum which is played while held under the armpit. The skin heads are fastened in place with cords which can be squeezed to change the pitch. It is exceptionally popular among the Yoruba who use it for communication, festivals, ceremonies, and recreation.

Danno
(gan-gan)

The edegere is a string of metal bells linked together on a hemp belt which is worn around the waist of the dancer. We first observed it in the Akabo Girls School, Nigeria. It is widespread and in one form or another used by both sexes and various age groups. The edegere sounds much like the rhythmic jingle of sleigh bells of the West.

Edegere

101

The ekwe was the most common instrument we came across on our expedition. It is the relative of the contemporary wood block and is played the same way. It is made from a relatively hard wood and can be found in most traditional orchestras.

Ekwe

Horns

These cone shaped metal horns are played by blowing through an aperture near the narrow end of the instrument. By using the thumb to open or close a hole located at the vertex of these horns, two pitches can be produced. Similar instruments are made of elephant tusks, the horns of antelope, domestic cattle, and wild buffalo. They are usually very ornate, come in many sizes, and can be found throughout West Africa.

102

This bongo sounding instrument was first heard by us accompanying Urhobo singers and dancers in Egun, Nigeria. It was used effectively as the musicians injected its high pitched off-beat rhythms against the voices of the ensemble.

Igede

In this example the knockers are made of hollowed out metal pipes. Generally, they are made of two hardwood solid round pieces of wood that are struck against each other in a steady rhythmic pattern. It is played the same way as the clave of Latin-American bands of North and South America and is a relatively common instrument.

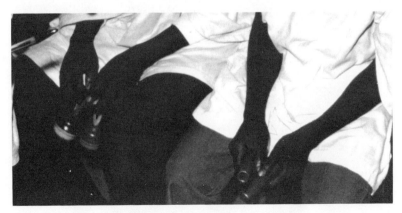

Knockers

103

The body of this instrument is made from the dried husk of a large hollowed-out gourd. A skin is stretched over the top and held in place by rawhide thongs affixed to a metal hoop at the bottom. The outer shell is covered with the hide of a

leopard, or painted a particular color depending on the tribal group. Its sound resembles that of the tenor drum. It is popular throughout Ghana and Togo and is used predominantly in combination with the danno in southern Ghana.

Mpintintoa

This is a xylophone-like instrument which spells out two octaves of a pentatonic scale. Its hardwood keys are held in place by pins which are driven into two thick trunks of banana palms. The total length of the instrument is from five to eight feet, and it is played by up to three musicians simultaneously. The master musician assumes the dominant role in the playing of the nglenge. It is found primarily in Nigeria and is very common among the Ibo, Imbibio, and Efik. The nglenge which we heard produced a perfect jazz blues scale.

Nglenge

This instrument can be seen in many shapes and sizes. They are all made of the same basic components — beads and a shell. Some have thier beads inside the shell while on others they are ornately strung on the outside. The shell of these maraca type instruments are made of gourds, woven bamboo or metal, and can be found in their various forms throughout West Africa.

Oshara

This plucked instrument is constructed in the shape of a cubicle. It has a hole in the top side which is covered with six metal prongs that spell out a pentatonic scale. In Abraka, Nigeria we witnessed the sologun in two sizes, the smaller (tenor sounding) two-foot version called the "small sologun" and the (bass) "big sologun" of 5 square feet.

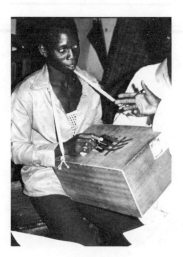

Sologun

105

The triangle can be heard in many areas of West Africa. We listened to its bell-like sounds in Gambia, Central Mali, Dahomey, Nigeria and Cameroon. Frequently it is made of scrap metals and is played the same way as the western triangle.

Triangle

The ubo, or as the Ibo of Nigeria call it, the local piano, is made of a hollowed-out calibash shell covered with a piece of straight soft wood. The two central holes are used to hold the instrument and amplify the sound of the chamber below. As in the sologun, this instrument has 6 prongs that produce a pentatonic scale. It is very popular among highlife musicians as it has a calypso type sound. In the traditional orchestra it is played by the master musician and can be heard all over Central Nigeria.

Ubo

The udu is found primarily in Nigeria and is especially used by the Ibos and Ijaws. These clay pots are struck across the mouth with the hand or a brush made of palm fronds (leafs). Water is added to change the pitch and tune the instrument. One drummer can play as many as four to six pot drums at a time.

Udu

107

Contemporary African Sculpture

Contemporary African Mosaic

109

7

AFRICAN MUSIC TODAY

When Louis Armstrong, the man whose broad beaming smile can be seen on Pepsi posters from the beaches of the Gulf of Guinea to the mud huts of Timbuktu, visited Africa in the late 50s, the Africans rolled out their best "high-life" bands and jazz musicians to play for him.

Louis, in a crushing response to the music of the people who had supplied the seeds which later turned into jazz, said, "Man, it just won't do."

Why the put down?

The African musicians that Louis heard were not relating instrumentally to the complex European harmonies found in jazz, just as early Europeans did not appreciate the complex forms and rhythms found in African music. They came from either a traditional urban or a transitional area which was in the throes of growing nationalism and development, and as a result, their music was in a state of flux.

While music in some of these remote villages has remained relatively unchanged, Western concepts of mass communication, education, law, technology and industrialization have affected the transitional and urban societies.

In urban areas there is a tendency to reject traditional music. This rejection comes primarily from individuals who are interested in "pop" and from those who have been exposed to Western education and culture and have cultivated a taste for classical music, religious hymns, and jazz. Traditional musicians, who come to the cities, are faced with the decision of adjusting to the musical demands of the new environment or changing their vocation to an avocation.

Even though traditional music continues to play an essential role in the lives of the people of the transitional areas, Western music has made an impact via radio, television, and motion pictures.

What did Louis hear? He heard traditional and local "popular" music, both of which contain Western and African elements.

In addition to a strong Anglo-American rock influence, much of the popular music that is heard is "high-life." High-life is a vocal calypso dominated style in combination with traditional music and jazz, primarily associated with good times and merry-making. Since the calypso music of the West Indies has its direct roots in West Africa and has remained in a purer state than the black man's music of America, it was easily assimilated back into West Africa. Of the foreign music played in Ghana and Nigeria, calypso is unquestionably most prevalent. It is the outgrowth of the African admiration for the exuberance, improvisation, and extensive use of percussion associated with American jazz.

High-life styles vary from country to country, place to place, and band to band in West Africa. Certain factors, however, have contributed to its development in all of the areas where it is found: radio, television, records, and motion pictures have disseminated music from other parts of the world; numerous young upper class Africans who frequently study abroad have cultivated tastes for Western music, particularly rock and jazz; and the combination of low prices with greater affluency have made Western instruments available to more people. These various influences stimulated experimentation by young people which led to the development of new musical forms.

High-life bands which use Western and African musical instruments, have become dominated by the sounds of the guitar. The guitar was introduced to Africa by the Spanish and Portuguese hundreds of years ago, but did not begin to become used widely in West Africa until the 1930s. Other Western instruments have been added along with traditional percussion instruments, such as the gan-gan.

Pidgin High-life uses "Pidgin English" which is spoken throughout Ghana and Nigeria. It is based on English with indigenous pronounciation and word usages.

Example:

"I go for im. I find im. I see im. Eee no day dare."

Translation:

"I went for him. I found that he wasn't there."

High-life bands are frequently composed of musicians from various tribal groups. In Nigeria it is very common to see Housa, Ibos and Yoruba playing together. The combination of the various tribal influences has undoubtably had a significant effect on the variations of high-life which have developed.

One example of a high-life variation with strong traditional emphasis is "Yoruba-juju" (not to be confused with witchcraft, but a rather interesting selection of words). In "Yoruba-juju," talking drums like the gan-gan dominate with the guitar playing a secondary role.

There is another less popular type of high-life called "blues," not to be confused with American jazz blues, since it does not contain the blues pitches, but is actually high-life played at a slower tempo.

High-life has been affected by social/environmental factors. High-life bands in the metropolitan areas perform at weddings, in ballrooms, hotels, nightclubs, and cafés. Town musicians perform at similar functions but to a lesser extent. Akin to the colorful mariachi bands of Mexico, early village bands helped to popularize "high-life" by taking their music to the streets. Today, street bands can be heard in the cities and towns all over West Africa.

Rural electrification and improved communications have changed the life styles and values of the African. In the process they have spread "high-life" throughout West Africa, making it unique in its intertribal distribution and acceptance. It has become the music of the Western conscious African sophisticates. Like the attitudes toward rhythm and blues, and jazz in America, many members of the older generation consider high-life a corruption of the established good, true, and beautiful. In spite of the nostalgic respect for the old, and the rising popularity of rock, high-life remains the popular music of the day.

Classical music is generally restricted to concert halls, churches, and educational institutions. It has a distinct African form, tends to be somewhat somber and structured and is not as popular as high-life. In 1933, noted African composer Dr. Ephraim Amu published a book of his compositions which were introduced through 80 important prelude exercises that were to influence African classical composers for generations. In his quest for new sounds, Dr. Amu adapted many European musical characteristics and combined them with African musical traditions (i.e., cross rhythms, rhythmic patterns, call and response, tonal and rhythmic correlation between words and melody, use of harmonic intervals, etc.).

Efforts are being made in the directions of classical music, theatre and dance in Ghana and Nigeria. This music contains the incipient elements for the emergence of a new and viable musical art form.

Modern African music has had a profound effect on the life styles of Africans. Jazz in America has had similar effects on the contemporary life styles of Americans. Many of these effects have been integrated into our culture to such a degree that most Americans fail to recognize its origins.

8

JAZZ – U.S.A.

If we agree that "americana" is the cultural behavior of America, then we must acknowledge that "americana" is influenced by jazz. When the novelist F. Scott Fitzgerald labeled the 1920s "The Jazz Age" he wasn't particularly interested in music. He was trying to describe a state of mind; a tempo and rhythm and a feel that was jazzy, and everyone understood what he meant.

> The restlessness approached hysteria. The parties were bigger. The pace was faster, the shows were broader, the buildings were higher, the morals were looser, and the liquor was cheaper; but all these benefits did not really minister to much delight. Young people wore out early—they were hard and languid at 21. Most of my friends drank too much—the more they were in tune to the times the more they drank. The city was bloated, glutted, stupid with cake and circuses, and a new expression 'Oh yeah?' summed up all the enthusiasm evoked by the announcement of the last super-skyscrapers.

> *(commentary on New York, 1926)*

JAZZ MUSIC

The channels through which jazz, near jazz and non-jazz (all called jazz) were heard, multiplied, rapidly as new media, such as the talking pictures, came into their own during the 20s.

The first sound movie, *The Jazz Singer*, starring Al Jolson, which opened in October 1927 and made millions for Warner Brothers, is a perfect example of jazz, really meaning the Jazz Age rather than jazz music. In spite of the title, any relationship between this film and jazz was purely coincidental. The nearest thing to jazz in the film is Jolson's marvelous whistling escapades which are certainly improvisation at its height. This important film raped the name jazz, made no reference to its African origins and utilized a white actor who did scenes in black face.

The expression "The Jazz Age" made musical sense too, for during the 20s jazz developed from infrequent musical performances in a few vaudeville acts to a household commodity. Phonograph records and the radio were probably the next most effective vehicles for the spreading of jazz. People throughout the U. S. were flocking to stores to buy the new talking machine with the big horn. The final irony was that the first recording of jazz was released by a white band, The Original New Orleans Dixieland Jazz Band, in 1917, symbolizing the continued exploitation of the black American's African heritage.

Because of this recording plus the endless numbers to follow by groups like King Oliver's Creole Band featuring Louis Armstrong, the Rhythm Kings, etc., white musicians such as Bix Beiderbeck started to listen to, became interested in, and shortly thereafter, started to play jazz.

DANCE

The black American's heritage is steeped in ritual, ceremonial, social and recreational dances, made up of free-flowing, energetic movements and steps which have easily adapted themselves to American dance.

115

African dance is very athletic and places great demands on the entire body. Even though there are cultural differences between tribes, there are a number of general characteristics in African dance:

1) Aside from moments when the dancer jumps, he moves with bent knees and the torso close to the ground,
2) individual movements of the hips, shoulders, buttocks, head, arms,
3) the shuffling of the entire foot along the ground,
4) the use of polyrhythms,
5) the combination of dance and music as a single entity,
6) the use of syncopated movements,
7) individualistic styles within a group.

Many of the characteristics are similar to those stressed throughout this book on jazz music.

Considering the cultural propensities described above, it is understandable that even though the Slave Laws of 1740 prohibited "the beating of drums, blowing horns or the like" for fear of arousing the slaves to insurrection, the slaves continued to dance as they prayed and played. They danced to the sounds of the banjo (an African instrument) and to the beat of each other's hand-clapping. The sounds of their own steps, as they shuffled and used heel and toe beats, provided them with a natural accompaniment. These improvisational steps were the first phase in the development of tap dancing.

The "minstrel show" began in 1830 when troubador Thomas D. Rice saw an old Negro tap dance to his own song and imitated him on the stage of a Louisville, Kentucky theatre the same evening.[1] Between the years 1840 and 1915 a number of all-black minstrel shows toured America, leaving their mark on the American musical comedy. Black dancers, stereotyped as "entertainers," were seen mainly in nightclubs and vaudeville houses until the 1920s when theatres finally welcomed them into the ranks of their reviews.[2]

America's most famous tap dancer, Bill Robinson, established his reputation in the Broadway production *Blackbirds of 1928*. Seven years later, George Gershwin confirmed the Afro-American as a legitimate performer when he created America's first folk opera, *Porgy and Bess*, successfully combining a black drama with song and dance. This work is certainly one of the most important operas of the 20th century.

Popular dances such as the Charleston, Cakewalk, Lindy Hop, Jitterbug and the Twist, are a direct or indirect outgrowth of specific African dance movements.[3] In the Charleston, for example, the use of hand crossing and uncrossing movements at the kneecaps are virtually unaltered from the African Juba dance.[4] In Lerone Bennet's book, *Before the Mayflower*, he talks about films shot in African villages showing perfect examples of the Charleston. The swaying motion of the Twist dates back to Africa and its displaced citizens within the South. Marshal Stearns talks of its movements in a song entitled *Ballin' the Jack*, written by two black Americans back in 1913 for the Ziegfield Follies; the great jazz pianist Jelly Roll Morton sang the words "Sis' . . . out on the levee doin' the double twis' " in the early 1900s in New Orleans; in the 20s, blues singers used it to accentuate their points as they shook their arms in counterpoint to their bodies while belting out many a jazz tune; and the 30s saw it again as partners separated in the break within the Lindy. Pure African dance movements became integrated into jazz and modern dance through the vehicle of "primitive dance."[5] The objective of primitive dance (led by dance historian/ choreographer Katherine Dunham and Mark Primus) was to expose African dance movements as an important and relevant idiom which could be incorporated into the wide spectrum of jazz and modern dance. Because of their work, a sincere interest was kindled and jazz dance became that much richer as a result of this ethnic integration.

Bill Robinson

Jazz dance went through an even greater revolution in the late 40s when it became influenced by modern dance. Modern dance introduced it to a new type of precise classical control and artistic professional quality that had been missing beforehand. Choreographers such as Donald McKayle went on to produce profound dance works with powerful social implications that have surprised the dance world since the 1950s. In *District Storyville*, he brings us back to the cradle of jazz at the turn of the century. The sounds of life are overshadowed throughout the work by an atmosphere of screaming brass and jazz drumming. The tempo of the work is astoundingly fast and the impact is astonishingly powerful. Within these works McKayle shows the obvious influence of Pearl Primus and primitive dance.

Alvin Ailey is probably one of the most exciting choreographers in America today. His works have been featured on TV, at theatres and universities throughout the world and have been an inspiration to a number of famous American composers, including Duke Ellington and Leonard Bernstein. Ailey's *Roots of the Blues* shows his deep involvement in jazz as a vehicle for expression.

Contemporary choreographers have been using the music of jazz artists in their dance since the 50s. The best known works of Talley Beatty (Road of the Phoebe Snow, Tango Place and Toccata) utilize the music of Miles Davis, Dizzy Gillespie, Duke Ellington and others. Eleo Pomare has utilized the music of Charlie Mingus, Oscar Brown, Jr., while Rod Rodgers has integrated the poetry of black writers such as Don L. Lee and Jackie Earley with the music of Yusef Lateef in his dance compositions.

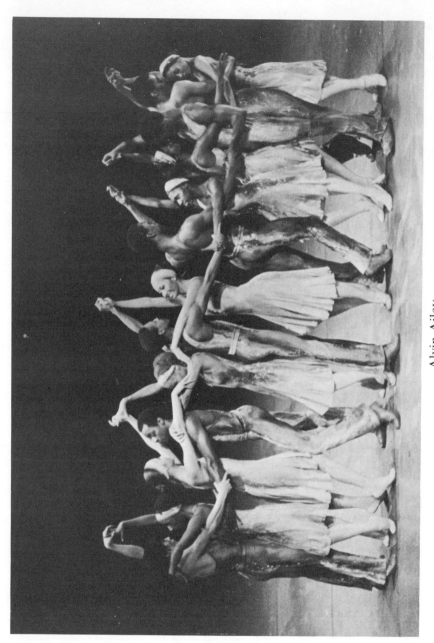

Alvin Ailey
From *Night Creature* to the music of Duke Ellington
photo by Fred Fehl

CLASSICAL MUSIC

It became apparent early in the 20th century that the infectious syncopated rhythms, drive and the magic of improvisation found in jazz would intrigue and influence the minds of many of the world's greatest contemporary composers.

From the teens through the 70s, encouraged by what jazz related to their ears and minds, composers of diversified backgrounds and temperament such as Ravel, Stravinsky, Weill, Poulenc, and Walton began experimenting with the blending of the blues, ragtime rhythms, improvisation and other jazz elements with traditional classical methods.

Darius Milhaud's composition *La Creation du Monde* begins with a prelude and fugue whose melody is reminiscent of Bach. The serene sounds of the melody are punctuated by a "lick" in the trumpets which indicates the direction of the work. This indication is soon confirmed by use of the flatted seventh, the roots of which go back to Africa, and trombone glissandos reminiscent of early slave field hollers. The double bass presents the theme of the jazz fugue, which is followed by the trombone, saxophone, and trumpet and eventually developed by the entire orchestra.

The work goes on to make excellent use of the blues, gives a feeling of group improvisation through a masterpiece of orchestration, and introduces sounds such as flute flutter-tonguing. *La Creation du Monde* is a charming, humorous, skillful work of refreshing originality which was to make a profound impression upon the musical world.

Igor Stravinsky once said that "he had a passion for jazz," and his works certainly reflected it. In 1918, when both the United States and Europe were on a ragtime craze, Stravinsky wrote *Ragtime for 11 Instruments*, including one that Leonard Bernstein called "that most unraggy Hungarian instrument—the cimbalom."[6]

The end result of this amalgamation of African derived jazz sounds and classical music is an impressive list of works that have given many concert-goers a pleasant and stimulating evening.

Ragtime for Eleven Instruments   *Igor Stravinsky*

A Selected List of Classical Composers Influenced by Jazz

Baker, David (1931—) *A Summers Day in 1945, Reflections*

Bernstein, Leonard (1918—) *Mass, West Side Story,*
    Concerto for Piano

Blitzstein, Mark (1905—1964) *The Cradle Will Rock*

Braine, Robert (1896—1940) *Concerto in Jazz*

Carpenter, John Alden (1876—1951) *Krazy Kat, Skyscrapers*

Chavez, Carlos (1899—1978) *Fox Blues*

Copland, Aaron (1900—) *Concerto for Piano and Orchestra,*
    Music For the Theatre

Cunningham, Arthur (1928—) *Ballet, Harlem Suite*

Foss, Lukas, (1922—) *Concerto for Improvising Solo*
    Instruments and Orchestra

Gershwin, George (1898—1937) *Rhapsody in Blue,*
    Concerto in F, Three Preludes, Porgy and Bess

Gould, Morton (1913—) *Choral and Fugue in Jazz,*
    Boogie Woogie Etude, Big City Blues,
    The Concerto for Tap Dancer and Orchestra

Grofe, Ferde (1892—1972) *Broadway at Night*

Kaufman, Fredrick (1936—) *The Nothing Ballet, Interiors*

Krenek, Ernst (1900—) *Johnny Spielt Auf*

Liebermann, Rolf (1910—) *Concerto for Jazz Band and*
    Orchestra

Milhaud, Darius (1892—1974) *Searamouche,*
    La Creation du Monde

Poulenc, Francois (1899—1963) *Rapsodie negre*

Ravel, Maurice (1875—1937) *Concerto for Left Hand,*
    Violin Sonata, Piano Concerto in G

Satie, Erik (1866—1925) *Parade*

Schuller, Gunther (1925—) *The Visitation*

Still, William Grant (1893—) *Afro-American Symphony*

Stravinsky, Igor (1882—1971) *Ragtime for 11 Instruments,*
    Ebony Concerto, Histoire du Soldat, Piano Rag Music

Walton, William (1902—) *Facade*

Weill, Kurt (1900—1950) *The Rise and Fall of Mahogony,*
    Three Penny Opera

Wilson, Olly (1937—) *Sometimes, Piece for Four*

ART

African art (paintings, face masks, staffs of office, carved thrones, etc.) is deeply tied to music and dance. Specific masks are carved and painted in a carefully prescribed manner for occasions like coronations, weddings, harvests, etc. These masks must be accompanied by the appropriate music. The use of art in African festivals is similar to that of the Mardi Gras of New Orleans.

African art has also made a profound impression on the paintings, sculpture and pottery of world renowned artists like Amadeo Modigliani and Pablo Picasso whose works reflect African artistic lines, color and composition.

Jazz itself is reflected in the works of many of the world's great artists. Painters such as Jackson Pollack, Andy Warhol, Franz Klein, Jasper Johns, Robert Indiana, Larry Rivers, Piet Mondrian, Stuart Davis, William de Kooning, Aaron Douglas, Archibald Motley, Robert Rosenquist and Roy Lichtenstein have all been influenced by it.

In 1940, with the war raging in Europe, Piet Mondrian moved to New York where the lights, color, tempo and jazz became the new loves of his late life. Mondrian, originally and temperamentally a Dutch landscape artist who was extremely sensitive to his surroundings, was overwhelmed by New York. He was inspired by the night lights of the sky-scrapers as they transformed themselves into brilliant blinking patterns of light and shadow. In the 1942 painting *Broadway Boogie Woogie*, one can almost read the blinking night facades on the office buildings and New York nightclubs. He reversed the process he had been involved in for years, the use of a black linear rectangular grid balanced against a color area. The grid now became the color area, with its lines containing red, blue and yellow squares. The off-white background gives the colors a feeling of vibration, creating the blinking light effect.

Mondrian's late jazz oriented works became a great inspiration to such painters as Stuart Davis (a devout jazz fan), Jackson Pollock, and William de Kooning.

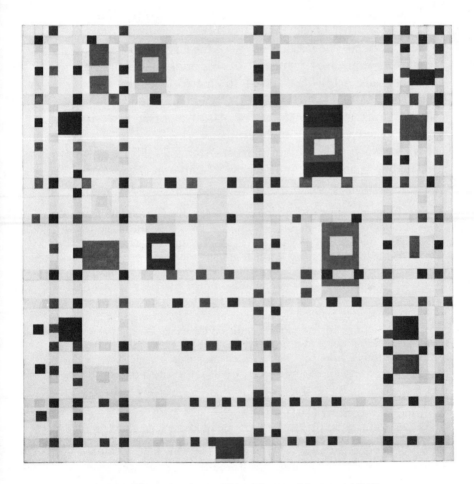

Piet Mondrian. *Broadway Boogie Woogie.* 1942

In Stuart Davis' paintings *Report From Rockport, The Mellow Pad* and *Rapt at Rappaport's*, the influence of jazz upon the artist is obvious both in his style and extensive use of jazz expressions. These paintings project abstract colored shapes, words, and jagged, twisted, vibrating lines that render the jazz style and pace of America in harmonic and dissonant colors.

During the 1920s a hopeful enthusiastic spirit among the black Americans gave birth to a movement called the Harlem Renaissance. The black man was beginning to be taken seriously. Social scientists were studying his society and he became the subject of a number of fine books and paintings. The most successful black artist to emerge from this movement was Aaron Douglas. His WPA commissioned large-scaled murals made good use of Afro-American historical themes as the basis for a number of his works.

When New Orleans born artist Archibald Motley was given a one man show at the New Galleries in New York, James V. Herring wrote:

> In his paintings of Voodoo mysteries, in the interpretations of modern American Negroes at play, in the weird allegorical canvases and in the portraits, Motley directly or by subtle indirection lays bare a generous cross-section of what psychologists call the subconscious—his own and that of his race. The ancient traits and impulses of his ancestors in Africa, Haiti, or wherever they found their habitation, are a milestone on the unending march; but the phantasmagoria bears the imprint of the modern molds into which so much of the old race-life has been poured. The same fundamental rhythms are found, whether the setting be a jungle presided over by witchcraft or a cabaret rocking to the syncopation of jazz.[7]

His paintings *Chicken Shack* and the *Jockey Club* certainly captured the spirit of Harlem in the 20s and 30s.

Andy Warhol, one of the leaders of the Pop Art movement in America, eventually became involved in jazz oriented improvisational movies and multi-media happenings along with artists such as Robert Indiana and Robert Raushenberg.

126

Aaron Douglas. *Aspects of Negro Life*, (panel 2, on slavery through Reconstruction), 1934. Oil on canvas, 4' 11" x 11' 8". Countee Cullen/Schomberg Collections (sponsored by the W.P.A.). New York Public Library (Astor, Lenox, and Tilden Foundations).

Aaron Douglas. *Aspects of Negro Life*, (panel 3, "The Idyll of the Deep South"), 1934. Oil on canvas, 4' 11" x 12'. Countee Cullen/Schomberg Collections (sponsored by the W.P.A.). New York Public Library (Astor, Lenox, and Tilden Foundations).

LANGUAGE

The American English language has become permanently painted with jazz expressions. Many of these expressions are linked to the manner in which the African slave developed his own unique accents and usage of the English language. He was suppressed by the white man and in order to communicate and survive forced to reject his own language, but still retained his musical affection for the spoken word. Under these pressures there emerged new speech patterns and cliches, which were eventually to be adopted into the jazz community as a whole. The following dialogue is typical of two BEBOPPERS in conversation during the 50s.

Musician #1: Say man whendya get the crazy cloth and the groovey lid?

Interpretation: Hello Henry. That's a lovely suit and hat you have on. When did you purchase it?

Musician #2: While gigging at Charlies. Say man, my choppers were right on that eve and the cats were really swinging.

Interpretation: I bought the clothing while working at Charlie's Nightclub. The band was excellent and I played very well that evening.

Musician #1: My ears have told me of a far out flick in town. How 'bout slipping into your spacepads, sippin' some seeds and splitting with me?

Interpretation: I heard that there is an interesting movie in the neighborhood. Why don't you put your shoes on, we'll have a cup of coffee and go to see it together.

Musician #2: Crazy, man, crazy!

Interpretation: Why, thank you, I would love to!

Many of the terms originated by the jazz community have been incorporated into the speech patterns of all Americans.

SCHOOLS

Jazz has had a broad impact on our society. Its influences envelope us. It has become a part of us.

Numerous black American scholars are eagerly documenting the various elements of the African heritage and its contributions to American culture. This has been responsible for the inclusion of courses on jazz in the curriculum of most colleges and universities. In some it might be a simple part of a black studies course, but more often it includes a complete class or course of study on the history of jazz. Some colleges have expanded their jazz curriculum to include courses in jazz arranging, scoring, composing, and improvisation. The Berklee School of Music in Boston is a four year college devoted exclusively to jazz, staffed with some of America's finest musicians and offers a degree in music.

College stage (jazz) bands dot the country from the Atlantic to the Pacific, with such schools as North Texas State University boasting of as many as 15 excellent jazz ensembles. State regional high school and college stage band contests have become commonplace. America's finest jazz orchestras and artists can be seen and heard giving workshops and concerts on campuses throughout the year.

Stage bands came to the public attention back in the 50s when Marshall Brown commissioned composers such as Don Sebesky and John LaPorta to write for his high school band. The end product was a series of high quality jazz arrangements that could be played at the high school, and in some cases even the junior high and elementary school levels, and still sound good. The compositions were graded from the very simple to the professional level and were the first of their kind in the country. Today, publishers such as Alfred, Kendor, Creative World, Berklee and numerous others produce interesting works that can be bought along with professional recordings to aid the director and their young musicians. Incidentally, Marshall Brown's high school band of the 50s was so good that they were invited to participate in the Newport Jazz Festival.

MASS MARKETS

College football half-time shows generally include large swinging college bands who put on a show that thrills thousands of people every weekend during the football season. The 1969 professional football Superbowl game in New Orleans included a half-time show that is hard to beat. As 30,000 people stood and cheered, jazz trumpet players Al Hirt and Doc Severenson "wailed" away on 15 foot high podiums at opposite ends of the field. They were accompanied by a 130 piece marching band spelling out the word JAZZ. All this was seen and heard over national television as millions of people watched.

Jazz became so big that the only place to move it was outdoors, and the jazz festival was born. The first big one and the father of them all was the Newport Jazz Festival. This was a very important development in the growth of musical culture in the United States. In this case, jazz, later rock and folk, were to become available to the mass public rather than the select few who could afford it. They started out as festivals in places like Newport, Concord, Monterey and culminated in Woodstock, where self-expression reached a new peak. Eventually, jazz found its way into the city streets of New York with the advent of the *Jazz Mobile.*

During the swing era (1935–1945), jazz musicians and bands rode a wave of popularity that produced competing fan clubs from one end of the country to the other. Jazz (in this case, swing) became for the first (and perhaps last) time, the pop music of the day. Swing was sold to America as a new kind of music. It was sold with all the new modern techniques of the press, the movies, the radio, on stage, at ballrooms and in juke boxes, as tons of new records were pressed each day.

The swing era produced a group of jazz fans, many of whom were college kids known as bobby-soxers. They loved their music hot, adored the big band sound and could afford to pay for it. They had their own language called jive talk and a swinging dance called the jitterbug.

131

The bands were so popular that people even imitated the musicians' stage dress, and in some cases exaggerated it. The end result was a new and short-lived phenomena called the "Zoot Suit." Even Al Capp in his cartoon Lil' Abner, could not resist introducing the zoot-suit.

The sounds of jazz have become an integral part of American television. In the 50s, programs such as Peter Gunn and M Squad employed jazz artists like Shelly Mann and singer Julie London as an integral part of their weekly serials. Today, television continues to utilize the sounds of jazz composers such as Henry Mancini, Lalo Shifrin, Neal Hefti, and Quincy Jones, in its specials, commercials, dramas, comedies and even children's cartoons.

Who could have predicted when witnessing a slave ship, slave auction, or workers in a cotton field, the potential impact these people were to generate out of such wretchedness and that something so creative, beautiful and important to our culture would evolve?

The American society has been unaware much too long of the pleasures it has accrued from the artistic contributions of black Americans while denying them recognition for the dominant role in the development of jazz. An America without jazz would not be the America we know today.

JAZZ–THE ONLY INTERNATIONALLY RECOGNIZED INDIGENOUS AMERICAN ART FORM!

NOTES

1. Walter Sorell, *The Dance Through the Ages* (New York: Grosset and Dunlap, 1967), p. 277.

2. Walter Terry, *The Dance in America* (New York: Harper and Brothers, 1958), p. 203.

3. Jean Sabatine, Jazz Dancing (Hoctor Dance Records, Waldwich, N.J., 1969), p. 12. These authors consider the word "primitive" as an unfortunate descriptive term, as it implies a lack of sophistication and backwardness.

4. Marian H. Winter, "Juba and American Minstelsy," *Chronicles of American Dance* (Watson Guptill Publications, New York, 1959), p. 40.

5. Langston Hughes, "The Negro and American Entertainment," *The American Negro Reference Book* (Englewood, N.J.: Prentice Hall, 1966), p. 831.

6. Leonard Bernstein, *The Infinite Variety of Music* (New York: Simon and Schuster, 1966), p. 54.

7. James V. Herring, "The American Negro as Craftsman and Artist" in Lindsay Patterson, ed., *The Negro in Music and Art* (New York: Publishers Company, 1963), p. 216.

BIBLIOGRAPHY

Ajayi, J. F. and **Crowder, M.** *History of West Africa.* J. W. Arrowsmith, Ltd., Bristol, 1971.

Akin, Euba. "The Dichotomy of African Music." *Courier Magazine.* UNESCO, Paris, *June 1973.*

Allen, W. F.; **Ware, C. P.**; and **Garrison, L. M.** *Slave Songs of the U.S.* A. Simpson and Co., 1967. Reprinted by Oak Publications, New York, 1965.

Arnason, H. H. *History of Modern Art.* Harry N. Abrams, Inc. Publishers, New York, 1970.

Basden, G. T. *Among the Ibo in Nigeria.* J. B. Libbineatt, Philadelphia, 1921.

Bebey, Francis. *African Music: A Peoples Art.* Lawrence Hill, New York, 1975.

Bernstein, Leonard. *The Infinate Variety of Music.* Simon and Schuster, New York, 1966.

Bogart, Max. *The Jazz Age.* Charles Scribner's Sons, New York, 1969.

Boulton, Laura. *Music Hunter.* Doubleday, Garden City, New York, 1969.

Brittannica Encyclopedia of Modern Art, The. Encyclopedia Britannica Educational Corp., Chicago, 1973.

Cable, G. W. "The Dance in Place Congo." *Century Magazine. February 1886.*

Cayou, Delores Kirton. *Modern Jazz Dance.* Mayfield Publishing Co., Palo Alto, 1971.

Charters, Samuel. *The Bluesmen.* Oak Publications, New York, 1967.

Courlander, Harold. *Haiti Singing.* Chapel Hill, University of North Carolina, 1939.

Cudjoe, S. D. "The Technique of EWE Drumming and Social Importance of Music in Africa." *Phylon # 16.* Atlantic University Press, 1953.

Curtin, Phillip D. *The Atlantic Slave Trade.* The University of Wisconsin-Madison, 1969.

Dance, Stanley. *The World of Swing.* Scribners, New York, 1974.

De Lerma, D. R. *Reflections on Afro-American Music.* Kent State University Press, 1973.

Ephson, Isaac S. *Ancient Forts and Castles of the Gold Coast.* Ilen Publishing Co., Ltd., Accra.

Field, M. J. *Religion and Medicine of the Ga People.* Crown
Agents, London, 1957.

Gamble, David P. "The Wolof of Senegambia." *Western
Africa, Part XIV.* London, 1957.

Ginsberg, Allen. *First Blues, Rags and Harmonium Songs
1971-74.* Full Court Press, New York.

Goffin, Robert. *Jazz.* Doubleday, Doran and Co., Garden
City, New York, 1944.

Gorer, Goeffrey. *African Dances.* Faber and Faber, London,
1935.

Green, Margaret M. *Ibo Village Affairs.* Sedwich and Jackson,
London.

Herring, James V. "The American Negro as Craftsman and
Artist." In Lindsay Patterson, edition, *The Negro in
Music and Art.* Publishers Company, New York, 1963.

Herskovits, M. J. *The Myth of the Negro Past.* Harper and
Brothers, New York, 1941.

Herskovits, M. J. and Herskovits, F. S. "The Outline of
Dahomey's Religious Beliefs." *American Anthropol-
ogical Studies.* Banta Publishing Company, Menasha,
Wisconsin, 1934.

Jones, A. M. *Studies in African Music.* Oxford University
Press, London, 1959.

Jones, LeRoi. *Blues People.* William Marrow and Company,
New York, 1963.

Kemble, Francis A. *Journal of a Residence on a Georgian
Plantation.* Harper and Brothers, New York, 1864.
Reprinted by Alfred Knopf, New York, 1961.

Kerouac, Jack. *Mexico City Blues.* Grove Press, New York,
1959.

Laeye, I. Timi of Ede, "Yoruba Drums." *Odu: Journal of
Yoruba's and Related Studies.* No. 7. Lagos, *March,
1959.*

Lomax, Alan. *Mister Jelly Roll.* Duell, Sloan and Pierce,
New York, 1950.

Lucas, J. Olumide. *The Religion of the Yorubas.* Lagos CMS
Bookshop, Lagos, 1948.

Melville, J. and Herskovits, F. S. *Dahomey: An Ancient West
African Kingdon.* 2 vols. Northwestern University
Press, Evanston, Illinois, 1967.

Merriam, Alan P. *The Anthropology of Music.* Northwestern
University Press, Illinois, 1964.

Merriam, A. P. "Music Bridge to the Supernatural." *Tomorrow's Magazine.* Vol. 5, No. 4, 1957.

Metrau, A. *Voodoo in Haiti.* Shocken Books, New York, 1972.

Morel, E. D. *The Black Man's Burden.* Modern Reader Paperback, New York and London, 1920.

Nadel, S. F. *The Black Byzantinium.* Oxford University, London, 1942.

Nettl, Bruno. *Folk and Traditional Music of the Western Continents.* Prentice Hall, New Jersey, 1973.

Nikiprowetzky, Iolia. "Les Griots du Senegal et Leurs Instruments." *Journal of the International Folk Council, XV.* Paris, 1963.

Nketia, Kwabena J. H. *African Gods and Their Music.* University of Ghana, Legon, 1970.

Nketia, Kwabena J. H. *Funeral Dirges of the Akan People.* University of Ghana, Legon, 1955.

Nketia, Kwabena J. H. *Ghana—Music, Dance and Drama.* Institute of African Studies, University of Ghana, Legon, 1965.

Nketia, Kwabena J. H. "The Role of the Drummer in Akan Society." *African Music.* 1954.

Nketia, Kwabena J. H. *The Music of Africa.* W. W. Norton, 1974.

Odum, H. W. and Johnson, G. B. *Negro Workaday Songs.* Chapel Hill: University of North Carolina Press, 1926.

Oliver, Paul. *Savannah Syncopators.* Studio Vista, London, 1970.

Parrinder, E. G. *West African Religion.* Epworth Press, London, 1949.

Patterson, Lindsay. *The Negro in Music & Art.* United Publishers Co., New York, 1970.

Polany, Karl. *Dahomey and the Slave Trade.* University of Washington Press, Seattle, 1966.

Rattray, R. S. *Ashanti.* Claredon Press, 1923.

Roberts, John S. *Black Music of Two Worlds.* Praeger, New York, 1972.

Sabatine, Jean. *Jazz Dancing.* Hector Dance Records, New Jersey, 1969.

Sargent, Winthrop. *Jazz: Hot and Hybrid.* E. P. Dutton and Co., New York, 1946.

Saxon, Dreyer and Tallent, ed. *Gumbo Ya Ya.* Houghton Mifflin Co., Boston, 1945.

Schuller, Gunther. *Early Jazz.* Oxford Press, New York, 1965.

Schwabs, George. "Tribes of the Liberian Hinterland." *Peabody Museum Papers.* Vol XXI. Harvard University, 1947.

Snide, G. T. and Ifeka, C. *Peoples and Empires of West Africa.* Thomas Nelson and Sons, Ltd., London, 1971.

Sorell, Walter. *The Dance Through The Ages.* Grosset and Dunlap, New York, 1967.

Southern, Eileen. *The Music of Black Americans: A History.* W. W. Norton and Co., Inc., New York, 1971.

Stearns, Marshall. *The Story of Jazz.* Oxford Press, New York, 1976.

Terry, Walter. *Dance in America.* Harper and Brothers, New York, 1958.

Tracy, Hugh. "The Development of Music in Africa." *Optima Magazine.* Vol. 14, # 1. *March, 1964.*

Wachsmann, Klaus P. *Essays on Music and History in Africa.* Northwestern University Press, Evanston, 1971.

Walker, Leo. *The Great Dance Bands.* Doubleday and Co., New York, 1972.

Walton, Dritz M. *Music: Black, White and Blue.* Morrow, New York, 1972.

Whorf, Benjamin Lee. *Language, Thought and Reality.* Massachusetts Institute of Technology, Cambridge, Massachusetts, 1964.

Work, J. W. *American Negro Songs.* Howell, Soskin and Co., New York, 1940.

Africa South of the Sahara. *(Folkways)* FE-4503
African and Afro-American Drums. *(Folkways)* FE-4502
African Drums. *(Folkways)* AB-4502
African Music. *(Folkways)* 8852
African Music from the French Colonies. *(Columbia)* SL-205
Afrique. *(Vogue)* EXTP-1029
Afrique Noire. *(Bam)* LD-409A
Anthology of Music of Black Africa. *(Everest)* 3254
Baoulé of the Ivory Coast. *(Folkways)* 4476
Cotê d'Ivoire - Dahomée - Guiñee *(Vogue)* MC-20-141
Ewe Music of Ghana. *(Folkways)* 4222
Field Recordings of African Coast Rhythms. *(Riverside)*
    RLP-4001
Folk Music of Ghana. *(Folkways)* FW-8859
Folk Music of Liberia. *(Folkways)* FE-4465
Folk Music of Western Congo. *(Folkways)* 4427
La Musique des Groits - Senegal. *(Ocora)* OCR-15
Music of the Idoma of Nigeria. *(Folkways)* FE-4221
Musiques Dahoméennes. *(Occra)* OCR-17
Negro Music of Africa and America. *(Folkways)* FE-4500
Ogoun Dieu du Fer (Ogun, God of Iron). *(Vogue)* LVLX-190
Pondo Kakou: Musique de Societe Secrete. *(Countrepoint)*
    MC-20141
Pygmies of the Ituri Forest - Congo, The. *(Folkways)*
    FE-4457
Something New from Africa. *(Decca)* LK-4292
Wolof Music of Senegal and the Gambia. *(Folkways)*
    FE-4462

AFRICAN MUSICAL INSTRUMENTS

Drums

Congo Drums. *(London)* LB-828
Drums of the Yoruba of Nigeria. *(Folkways)* 4441
Haute - Volta. *(Ocora)* SOR-10
Music of the World's Peoples. *(Folkways)* FE-4504
Musique Kongo. *Ocora)* OCR-35
Percussions - Afrique No. 1. *(Ocora)* OCR-39

Keyboard Instruments
> Haute - Volta. *(Ocora)* SOR-10
>
> Musical Instruments II: Reeds. *(Gallotone)* GALP-1323
>
> Musical Instruments V: Xylophones. *(Gallotone)* GALP-1326
>
> Musique Du Cameroun. *(Ocora)* OCR-25
>
> Musique Kabre du Norde - Togo. *(Ocora)* OCR-16

String Instruments
> Anthologie de la Musique du Tchad. *(Ocora)* OCR-38
>
> Haute - Volta. *(Ocora)* SOR-10
>
> Musique Kongo. *(Ocora)* OCR-35
>
> Niger, la Musique des Groits. *(Ocora)* OCR-20
>
> Senegal, La Musique des Groits. *(Ocora)* OCR-15

Wind Instruments
> African Coast Rhythms: Tribal Folk Music of West Africa. *(Riverside)* RLP-4001
>
> Anthologie de la Musique des Groits. *(Ocora)* OCR-38
>
> Anthologie de la Musique du Tchad. *(Ocora)* OCR-37
>
> Baoule of the Ivory Coast. *(Folkways)* FE-4476
>
> Haute - Volta. *(Ocora)* SOR-10
>
> Musical Instruments II: Reeds. *(Gallotone)* GALP-1323
>
> Musique Kabre du Norde - Togo. *(Ocora)* OCR-16
>
> Musique Kongo. *(Ocora)* OCR-35
>
> Tangayika Territory. *(London)* LB-567

INDEX

References to drawings are printed in boldface type. Numbers in italics refer to the photographic inserts; the first number is that of the location (plate no.) of the insert, the second that of the page in the insert

141

143

144

145

146

CONTENTS OF 2 – 7" – 33 1/3 RPM RECORDINGS

Records included in hard cover edition.
Also available separately from the publisher.

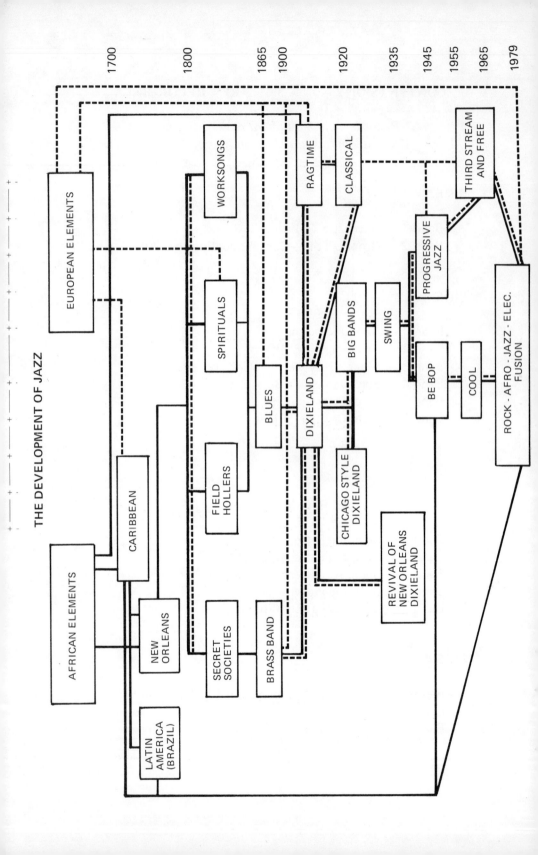

THE DEVELOPMENT OF JAZZ

1700 1800 1865 1900 1920 1935 1945 1955 1965 1979

EUROPEAN ELEMENTS

WORKSONGS

RAGTIME

CLASSICAL

THIRD STREAM AND FREE

SPIRITUALS

PROGRESSIVE JAZZ

BIG BANDS

SWING

BLUES

DIXIELAND

BE BOP

COOL

ROCK - AFRO - JAZZ - ELEC. FUSION

FIELD HOLLERS

CHICAGO STYLE DIXIELAND

REVIVAL OF NEW ORLEANS DIXIELAND

CARIBBEAN

AFRICAN ELEMENTS

NEW ORLEANS

SECRET SOCIETIES

BRASS BAND

LATIN AMERICA (BRAZIL)